On Target in Children's Church

On Target
in Children's Church

by

Ruth E. Gibson

Beacon Hill Press of Kansas City
Kansas City, Missouri

Cover Art: Royce Ratcliff

Permission to quote from the following copyrighted versions of the Bible is
acknowledged with appreciation:

The Holy Bible, New International Version (NIV), copyright © 1978 by the
New York International Bible Society.

The *New Testament in Modern English* (Phillips), Revised Edition © J. B.
Phillips, 1958, 1960, 1972. By permission of the Macmillan Publishing Co.

10 9 8 7 6 5 4 3 2 1

Lovingly dedicated
to
my son, Charles W. Gibson,
and to
my daughter, Carolyn R. Vance

Contents

Foreword

You are holding one of the most complete children's church manuals available—*On Target in Children's Church.* Ruth E. Gibson, its author, is an experienced leader in this field of ministry. From 1972-80 she served the Church of the Nazarene as general director of Children's Church. During that time she traveled widely, training children's workers. Now she has written this handbook to help those who have been called by God and the church to serve in this ministry.

On Target in Children's Church is a practical book. Mrs. Gibson shares scores of ideas that will help you provide profitable worship experiences for the children of your church. She begins by showing why children's church is worth your time and effort. Then she discusses the place of music, the Bible, prayer, storytelling, discipline, and evangelism in children's church. Throughout she makes it clear that a successful program requires commitment and hard work.

You will enjoy Ruth Gibson's inspirational writing style. This is not a dry technical text but a living guide filled with illustrations. If you follow the course outlined here, you will be— *On Target in Children's Church.*

MARK A. YORK
Children's Ministries

Acknowledgments

Nothing is ever accomplished without the creative involvement and support of other people. I would like to briefly acknowledge my gratitude to the following:

- My husband, who accepted my late hours at work with only a degree of displeasure and encouraged me to try;
- Miriam Hall, who, as Children's Ministries director, gave me the opportunity to write this book;
- Mark York and Jeannette Wienecke, who sent verbal messages often that encouraged me to believe I could write.
- C. Ellen Watts, Robert D. Troutman, Dr. Earl Wolf, and Dave and Janet Anderson for their writings in the *Edge* magazine.
- All who have given me the gifts of information, insights, advice, and vicarious experience through articles, books, and active participation in workshops across the nation.

Also deeply appreciated are:

- Robert D. Troutman, who as editorial director in Children's Ministries, did the final editing;
- Mark York, who as Children's Church general director, recognized this book's value and saw it through to production.

PART I

GET READY—Know

Sculpture

I took a piece of plastic clay,
And idly fashioned it one day,
And as my fingers pressed it, still
It moved and yielded to my will.

I came again when days were past:
The bit of clay was hard at last.
The form I gave it still it bore,
And I could fashion it no more.

I took a piece of living clay,
And gently pressed it day by day
And moulded it with power and art
A young child's soft and yielding heart.

I came again when years were gone:
It was a man I looked upon.
He still that early impress bore,
And I could fashion it no more!

—Author unknown

1

The "WHAT" and "WHY" of Children's Church

There is more going on in children's church than you may realize. Searching minds and tender hearts are receiving never-to-be-forgotten impressions. Planned learning and worship experiences, plus your Christian example, are influencing children's lives and relationships with God.

Albert Lown tells the story of a great sculptor named Johann Dannecker. He was well known for his statues, especially those of Grecian goddesses. As he neared middle age, he realized that although he had been quite successful, he had not created a masterpiece. He set about to do so, choosing as his subject the figure of Christ.

Dannecker worked long and thoughtfully. One day he invited some children to view the statue. They stood before the figure and looked intently at it.

"Who do you think it is?" asked Dannecker.

"It is a good man," answered the children.

The sculptor's disappointment was apparent. He had hoped they would recognize it to be Christ. When the children were gone, he took up his tools and continued to work.

After some time, he invited the children to come again. Once more he asked, "Who do you think it is?"

"It is a very good man," they answered.

Disappointed again, Dannecker went back to work.

He brought the children back the third time and asked, "Who do you think it is?"

"IT IS JESUS!" they chorused.

"Jesus it is," said Dannecker. The figure was taken from his studio and gained a place among the great statuary of the time.

Not long after this, the Emperor Napoleon sent for Dannecker.

"Come to Paris," said Napoleon. "I want you to make a statue of the goddess Venus for the Louvre."

Dannecker declined the invitation though he knew it would mean great honor.

"Sire," he said to Napoleon, "the hands that carved the Christ can never again carve heathen goddesses."

There is a similarity between sculpting a statue and shaping the eternal destiny of a child. Once you have caught a vision of the sacredness of your task, no lesser endeavor will ever seem equal to it. An unknown poet expressed it well in these words:

> They pass so quickly, the days of youth,
>   and children change so fast;
> And soon they harden in the mold,
>   And the plastic years are past.
>
> So we shape their lives while they are young,
>   This be our prayer, our aim;
> That every child we touch shall bear
>   The imprint of His name.

What Is Children's Church?

To better understand the value of children's church, let's examine the WHAT and WHY of this special ministry.

Children's church is a worship program that—
    (1) is designed especially for children.
    (2) uses concepts children can understand.
    (3) relates the Bible to life.
    (4) should be filled with variety.
    (5) involves children physically, mentally, and spiritually.

Children's church is not just another Sunday School session. It is not entertainment, busywork, or baby-sitting. Children's church is a time of worship!

Children's church does not include toddlers, twos and threes, or kindergarten children. These younger boys and girls should be involved in extended session programs for their age-groups. Extended session instructional materials are found in the *Toddler Teacher, Twos and Threes Teacher,* and the *Kindergarten Teacher.*

The Why of Children's Church

Examining each part of the definition of children's church will help to bring the "WHY" into focus.

Children's Church Is Designed Especially for Children

Have you ever watched the children in your congregation during the worship service? Some make paper airplanes out of the bulletins. Some play ticktacktoe on the hymnals. Others avoid sitting still by wearing a path to the rest room.

Why do children do these things? It's not because the pastor is a poor preacher. It's not because children are disrespectful or disobedient. The real reason is that a service geared to adults does not meet the needs of children. Because of this lack, the

17

children not only learn inappropriate behavior but also may develop strong negative feelings against church. They may begin to associate church and the Christian life with boredom and stern suppression.

A worship service designed especially for children is exciting because it meets their needs. It lessens the risk of "immunizing" them against worship. Many adults who learned to "turn off" the message as a child have never since found the "on" button!

Children's Church Uses Concepts Children Can Understand

Children think concretely. The symbolic language commonly used by adults may conjure up strange images in a child's mind. In children's church we can take the time and use activities that help us check what the children are really learning.

One children's church director was presenting a unit on the Ten Commandments. In one of the activity times, she asked each child to choose a commandment and draw a picture to explain its meaning to the other children. Here is what one third grader drew to explain the third commandment:

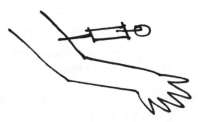

It is obvious that this child's experience had not included an explanation of the word *vain*. In school he had learned about the veins and arteries of the body. With the limited knowledge he had, how else could he have visualized "THOU SHALT NOT TAKE THE NAME OF GOD IN VAIN" but to put God in a needle and inject Him into a vein?

Of course the teacher explained the correct meaning of the

commandment. Children's church allows time to check what the children are learning and provides time for extended explanations necessary to correct mistaken concepts.

Children's Church Relates the Bible to Life

Every children's church session should be planned to give the child something he can put into practice in his own life. We cannot be sure children have learned Christ's way until we see them living it.

In *Abundant Living,* E. Stanley Jones says, "You know as much as you are willing to put into practice, and *no more."* Although he was talking about adults, the same is true about children. Only when a Bible truth expresses itself in a changed life has learning taken place.

When you prepare a children's church session, read the scripture passage carefully two or three times. Then ask yourself the following questions:

1. What does the passage say? What message is the writer trying to get across?

2. What does it mean? What principles are being taught? Can a child understand it? When a child can take a Bible truth, personally think it through, and then express that truth in his own words, he has begun to learn.

3. How does it apply to life? Think of the needs of the children. What can they do in their lives to live the truth the scripture teaches?

In children's church use activities that help the child begin practicing spiritual principles. One way to do this is to give each child a copy of the Bible verse he studied. Encourage him to keep a record of the number of times he uses the verse during the week. Ask the children to bring the verse card back and tell about a time they put it into practice. This sharing time could be a regular part of each Sunday's transition activities.

Children's Church Should Be Filled with Variety

Children's church does not have to be boring to be good. In fact, if it is boring, it is not good!

Do not be satisfied with shopworn methods or lusterless approaches. The biblical message is changeless, but teaching methods must be constantly changing.

There are many ways to present Bible truth so it catches and keeps attention. Many of these methods are written into the children's church materials. However, you will also want to use teaching techniques you have developed for your particular group of children.

Select a teaching method that promotes the particular types of learning you want.

Do you want the children to learn facts? Consider using Bible games.

Do you want them to understand the meaning of a Bible story? Try role playing, creative writing, or drawing.

Do you want the children to apply biblical truth to their own lives? Involve them in service projects.

To insure variety, each part of the service must be closely coordinated. The planned activities should fill the allotted time. Never should the leader have to ask, "What do you want to do now?" Children are scarcely equipped to do the leader's planning!

Another important part of variety is eye appeal. Be lavish with visual aids. A single picture is better than nothing, but imagination plus flannelgraph, filmstrips, puppets, flash cards, or chalk art can work wonders. None of these is magic. It is *you* who must use them to make the truth "come alive" for children.

Variety does not mean an unpredictable order of service so that children never know what to expect. Balance consistency of format and variety of methods to make children's church enjoyable.

Children's Church Involves Children Physically, Mentally, and Spiritually

Meaningful involvement is an essential factor in most learning. Unless children participate actively, they will not learn much, and both leaders and children may be just wasting their time.

The following is an account of how children were involved in one children's church:

"Our expanded bus ministry created new opportunities and problems. In a survey, we found that nearly one-half of the children had never attended an adult worship service. The simple solution would have been to take the children to the adult worship service and expose them to that experience. But first, they needed to learn how to worship. We decided to have the children make a slide series on 'Worship.'

"The project took four Sundays. The first Sunday the group discussed the question 'What does coming to church mean to you?' Then the children drew a mural depicting their conclusions.

"The second Sunday, the topic was 'What does the word *worship* mean to you?' The children made posters illustrating their answers.

"On the third Sunday, the discussion focused on elements of a worship service. We made slides of children posing the different parts of the service. Each major division of the worship service was called a 'scene.' Each child selected a piece of paper from a cup, which indicated the scene in which he would appear.

"Taking pictures of 2 or 3 children while another 30 waited their turn seemed to invite problems. We tried to prevent them rather than deal with them after they occurred. After explaining carefully what we were planning to do, we asked the children for help and cooperation. We said, 'When 1 or 2 children are having their pictures taken, everyone else will be in the background. We want you to look as if you were in an actual church service.'

Three chairs were placed in the back of the room for anyone who did not cooperate!

"In the 40-50 minutes it took to shoot the 42 slides, there was complete cooperation. The children had also taken a giant step toward learning to worship. They had participated."

A discussion of the "WHY" of children's church would not be complete without looking at our goals.

1. To win unsaved children to Christ.

2. To teach children how to worship and provide appropriate worship experiences.

3. To help children understand and appreciate God's Word.

4. To guide children to put biblical truths into action in their lives.

5. To develop the spiritual potential of each child.

6. To build strong Christian relationships between the worker and the child, and the child and his peers.

7. To help children develop positive attitudes toward the church.

8. To teach reverence toward God.

9. To help children participate in Christian service.

10. To provide children with Christian fellowship.

11. To prepare children to participate meaningfully in adult worship services.

12. To enlarge the children's vision for world mission.

In Children's Church We Take Shorter Steps

Today, my daughter wears a size seven shoe. But I can remember when size one fit her perfectly. When we walked together then, I slowed my pace because it took her many small steps to keep up with me. Today, our strides match almost exactly.

In children's church, we walk with the child toward spiritual understanding at his natural pace. The child's ability to grasp spiritual truth may be delayed if he has to stretch for that truth in an adult worship service. He may sit Sunday after Sunday failing to comprehend most of the service because no one thought to take shorter steps so he could follow.

In children's church, we slow our steps deliberately to show children the way. Easy? Not always. Rewarding? You can count on it!

The Soul of a Child

The soul of a child is the loveliest flower
    That grows in the garden of God.
It climbs from weakness to knowledge and power
    To the sky from the clay and the clod.

To beauty and sweetness it grows under care,
    Neglected 'tis ragged and wild;
'Tis a plant that is tender and wondrously rare,
    The sweet wistful soul of a child.

Be tender, O gardener, and give it its share
    Of moisture, of warmth, and of light;
And let it not lack painstaking care
    To protect it from frost and the blight.

A glad day will come when its blooms shall unfold.
    It will seem that an angel has smiled,
Reflecting a beauty and sweetness untold
    In the sensitive soul of a child.

In the breast of a bulb is a promise of spring;
In the little blue egg is a bird that will sing;
In the soul of the seed is the hope of the sod;
In the soul of a child is the kingdom of God.

                    —Author unknown

CHAPTER 2

Know the Child

In children's church, your assignment is to present God and His Word to children. To do this, you must know them both well.

Know the Child's Needs

Children come in all shapes, sizes, colors, and abilities. In spite of these individual differences, there are some needs common to all children.

Children must know they are loved, no matter what! Your love must not be conditioned on good behavior. A child requires love most when he is unlovely or in trouble. Express love through a pat on the shoulder, with a ready smile, by taking time to listen, or by a hug. "This is neat," said one child after a busy session. "You find things out here, and people like you."

Children need a good self-image. Everything a child does is colored by his feelings about himself. Ridicule and sarcasm produce feelings of inferiority and are never appropriate. Let each child see in your eyes, hear in your words, and sense from your actions that he is a person of worth to you and to God.

Children need to be accepted as they are—not as you want them to become. Children are greatly influenced by the experiences life has handed them. They are not to be judged, but accepted. Change will come as you minister to them, including the ministry of acceptance.

Children need approval. Just as children need to accept their own worth, they long to have their peers and the adults in their lives consider them to be of value.

Children need security. They need to know children's church is a safe place to be. If a problem arises, they should be able to count on a trusted worker to be there to help. Children also need the security of familiar routines: knowing what to do, how to do it, and when to do it.

Children need consistent control. A child must know his limits in order to feel secure. Every child should know what conduct is expected and that he will bear the consequences when rules are broken. He should not get away with something one Sunday and then be punished for the same thing later.

Children need to experience success. Success comes in many forms. It may come in a project that is challenging but still within reach. It may come in overcoming a behavior problem. It may come in learning Bible truths. Whatever its source, help the child as needed until he experiences success. Building patterns of success will help the child succeed in living a victorious Christian life.

Children need spiritual guidance. They need direction as they struggle with temptations that yesterday's children never faced. They need to know that God loves them and that forgiveness is available. The children's church worker who fails to give the spiritual guidance that leads to salvation and a victorious Christian life fails his children and God.

The time is right for these young ones to be shown the way to new life in Christ because . . .

1. Their minds are open and receptive.

2. Their desire to know is at a high peak; they are searching for answers.
3. Their lives are not yet cluttered by the tyranny of adult sins.
4. Their ability to trust and believe is unhindered by intellectual doubts. Jesus said, ". . . Except ye be converted, and become as little children, ye shall not enter into the kingdom of heaven" (Matt. 18:3).
5. Their response to the overtures of the Holy Spirit is simple, sincere, and quick.
6. Children are eager for guidance. Adults often have closed minds and inflexible attitudes, but children are ready followers.
7. The heart of a child is tender and his faith is simple. He has a spontaneity and freshness that makes his reaction pure and wholesome. The ability to respond with his whole being is one reason the child can make the leap of faith and come to know God in a genuine experience of conversion. (See *How to Lead a Child to Christ,* Chapter 14.)

Know the Child's World

The world is changing at an incredible rate. Today's child faces a world far different from that of even a generation ago. We must understand the world in which he lives, because its influence comes to church with him. Your knowledge of the child's world will heighten your understanding of the child himself and strengthen your ministry to him.

Television. The amount of time children spend watching television varies greatly from child to child and from home to home. The unwholesome influences of TV can be deterred where it is carefully monitored by parents. When this guidance is missing, children are prey to the influence of programs with questionable moral standards. Excessive television watching replaces other valuable activities such as family talks, games, outings, and even arguments that help children become mature individuals.

Books and magazines. Many homes have books and magazines that glorify violence or sex. When children have access to these, their morals are negatively influenced.

Music. Today, as never before, children hear and sing lyrics that contain immoral messages and suggestive phrases.

School. Public education is seen by many to be in crisis. Often there seems to be no clear conception of the school's goals and purposes. Traditional values have come under increasing fire and are being subtly replaced with secular humanism. In some instances educational technology and "burned-out" teachers have negated healthy personal relationships between children and teachers.

Mobility. Each year more and more families uproot and move to new communities. Children develop feelings of insecurity and the stability of family life is affected. Many families fail to find a church home in their new location.

The family. The trauma of divorce touches more than 25 percent of American homes. As a result, single-parent families are growing in number, and parents are marrying more than once. In almost half the homes with children under 18, both parents now work. These factors highlight the dramatic changes in the family structure that have occurred in recent years.

Money. Money is a tool most children know how to use well. Yet few grasp its value. Having been reared in times of plenty, many children are unfamiliar with thrift.

Today's children are caught in a storm of unrest. All the things mentioned above have a penetrating effect on them. They have no place to hide. They have no place to stop and rest. Life pushes them on. The world in which they live is different from the world in which we grew up. In children's church we need to be aware of these differences and minister with understanding.

Know the Child's Age Characteristics

The ages of the children with whom you work will determine the age level characteristics you will need to know well. The Church of the Nazarene Continuing Lay Training program has training texts to help you understand and work effectively with children of every age level. These books describe the child in detail, but there are some general characteristics for each age.

The kindergarten child. The kindergarten child is an imitator. His short attention span requires a variety of experiences to keep his interest. He is curious and uses all five senses to explore his world. Since he understands everything he hears in literal terms, he is easily confused by adult symbolism.

The primary child. This age child has a "built-in" wiggle. Someone has said, "I tell him to sit still and God tells him to wiggle. He listens to God rather than me." This does not mean that the leader should tolerate disorderly and irreverent behavior. It does mean that the program must be planned to allow the child to change positions frequently.

The primary's attention span is short—generally only six or seven minutes. Therefore, long Bible messages are inappropriate.

The primary child is full of energy and needs to be active. He likes to cut and paste. He is learning to read and enjoys using his new skill. Most children of this age need guidelines on how to get along with others.

Primary age boys and girls experience feelings of reverence and worship. Their emotions are easily seen and adult approval is important to them. They are known for their simple trust in God. Prayer time is very meaningful for them.

The middler child. Middlers are experiencing steady growth in every way. Their attention span is increasing, but they are not yet ready for long periods of sitting. The eight- and nine-year-old is developing the skills he acquired as a primary. He takes pleasure in reading the Bible. This group is greatly influenced by their peers, but they still respond to subtle adult guidance.

Middlers are growing in the knowledge of right and wrong, but they sometimes find it hard to admit to wrongdoing.

They can understand the nature of sin and the plan of salvation. Many may be ready to accept Jesus as their Savior. They all need to feel God's love and know they are important to Him.

The junior child. Juniors are generally healthy and energetic. They would much rather talk, read, or listen than work. They experience mood swings but generally are cooperative. Juniors want to know the reasons for right and wrong. They need to be permitted to make choices with as little help as possible. This encourages them to develop self-direction. Like middlers, juniors are strongly influenced by their peers. They like to compete in team games and take part in group activities. Many juniors memorize scripture easily, but they need help in understanding its meaning and how to apply it to their lives. Many juniors accept Christ as Savior.

Know Each Child Individually

Knowing the general characteristics of children at specific ages allows you to tailor your children's church sessions to meet the needs all children share. But just as no two snowflakes are the same, no two children are identical. They look different, they have different backgrounds and heredity, and each child's personal experiences are unique to him.

It is important that you do not consider children as a group. You must see individual boys and girls, each with his own strengths and weaknesses. As you understand each child, you will be better able to share Christ with him.

Below is a list of information you should know about each child.

1. His full name, home address, and telephone number. A child's name is important to him. Learn it quickly and use it often.

2. His age and birthday.

3. His grade in school.

4. His personal relationship with God.
   Is he a Christian? When did he accept Christ?
   Does he read his Bible regularly?
   Does he attend church regularly?
   Does his life give evidence that he is a growing Christian?

5. His home situation.
   Are his parents Christians?
   What is the quality of his homelife?

6. His self-concept. Does he perceive himself to be smart? dumb?

7. His relationship with his peers.

8. His special abilities and interests.
   What does he like to do? What can he do best?
   What does he resist doing? Do you know why?
   What distracts him? If he causes trouble, what happens immediately before the incident?

9. His hobbies and favorite entertainments.

10. His favorite television and sports personalities.

How Can I Get to Know a Child?

You can learn some things simply by asking for the information. Direct questioning, however, is not always the best way to learn what you need to know. It is a good idea to keep a notebook handy, with a page for each child, where you can record the information you discover.

Talk with the child. As you begin a new church year, or whenever you have a new group of children, use the first few Sundays as "get-acquainted Sundays." Begin by telling the children your name and a little about yourself. Then let them ask any questions they might have. As you share yourself, the children will find it easier to tell about themselves.

One way to encourage the children to tell about themselves is to play a game called "Interview." Ask questions such as:

What are some of your favorite things?

If you could go anywhere in the world, where would you go? Why?

What would you like to learn how to do?

When are you happiest?

What do you like to do when you have a day off school?

What part of children's church do you like best?

You could then turn to an activity. Ask them to draw a picture of a happy or a sad day; of something they like or something they don't like. As the children talk, make notes in your personal notebook or have a helper do this.

Private, individual conversation will also help you learn about a child. Such conversations are a good time to find out about his relationship with God.

Listen. Really listen! Give children an opportunity to express themselves. Hearing requires no effort—sound waves simply enter our ears. By contrast, creative listening is hard work. If you do listen, you can discover what children are thinking—and what their needs are.

A listening leader is one who responds to what the children say with his whole being. He listens with his heart as well as his mind. Active listening is one of the best ways to build a child's self-concept.

Observe. Look at the faces of the children you minister to. Are they happy or sad? What kind of day have they had so far? If something is bothering them, find out what it is. Be sure to notice new shoes, bumps and bruises, and moods. Comment accordingly. Children like to be recognized as persons of worth. Your observation will let them know you care.

Visit. You cannot really know the child without seeing him in his home setting. When he comes to children's church, every child brings his background—family, home, economic conditions, concern of parents. These are powerful influences on his behavior. You will be able to minister to the child better when you know "where he's coming from."

Find time for informal fellowship. A party is fun if the crowd is not large. Saturday parties for the whole group or Sunday dinner for a few enable you to see the children under less formal, "fun" conditions.

Game activities on Sunday morning are a good way to find out what each child knows about the Bible. Here is one game idea. Prepare six jigsaw puzzles by cutting apart pictures of six Bible persons. Have the child put a puzzle together and then write the individual's name and some pertinent facts about him. After completing one puzzle, he can proceed to the next, continuing until all have been used. You may be amazed at how much—or how little—some children know about the Bible. This information will help you be a better leader.

Talk with others who know the child. Sunday School teachers, public school teachers, and the pastor can help you understand your children. Be cautious of negative opinions, however. Give each child the benefit of the doubt.

Pray. Pray for each child individually. To do this, you need to know more than just his name and age. Get to know each child's needs. Remember, he is a unique person, different from every other child. Ask God to help you reach out to him as an individual. When he realizes that you love him, he will find it easier to feel that Jesus loves him and wants to be his Savior.

Young Feet Marching

It is the morning of life, and young feet are
    marching.
Hear the quick rhythm of their steps!
"Where are you going, children?" the leader
    asks.
A child has no words to reply; but faith
    looks out of clear eyes and answers
    confidently, "We are marching into
    tomorrow."
"And what of tomorrow—do you fear the
    unknown?"
"No, we do not fear, for everything
    concerning tomorrow lies *in your*
    hands—and God's.
We follow you who are older and wiser.
Surely you will not fail us, for you alone can
    guide us on the path of righteousness;
The way that will lead us safely through all
    the unknown years—
      ALL THE WAY TO GOD."

              —*Kathryn Blackburn Peck*

CHAPTER 3

The Leader's Qualifications

The future of the Church
is in the hands of children
　　　for they will lead the Church tomorrow!
The future of the Church
is in *your hands*
　　　as you minister to children today!

Perhaps no other person outside the home has more influence on the child than those who teach him. Theirs is an awesome responsibility. Those who teach children should be among the very best of the congregation, for Christian teaching demands that the teacher BE what he teaches. A teacher may teach mathematics and defraud the government on his income taxes. One may teach social studies and be unfaithful to his wife. He may teach economics and gamble away his earnings. But the person who accepts the responsibility of ministering to children in children's church cannot separate his teaching from WHO and WHAT he is.

What should we look for when we recruit a leader for children's church?

The Children's Church Worker Must Be—

A Growing Christian

The leader must KNOW Jesus Christ as his personal Savior. Only as he experiences the reality of God in his own life can he share that reality with children.

The children's church leader needs more than a one-time experience with God. He must be a growing Christian. Spiritual growth follows much the same pattern as physical growth. The human body needs a proper balance between nourishing food and adequate exercise. The spirit needs a proper balance between the spiritual food of God's Word and the exercise of Christian service.

A Living Example

The leader *must be the kind of person* he wants the children to become. He should give evidence that God is at work in his life. In a lecture at Nazarene Theological Seminary, Dr. Howard Hendricks said, "We teach best by consistent example." He cited research conducted at Stanford University that suggests modeling may be one of the most effective teaching methods known.

What the leader is, the children will learn. As he lives out the Word of God, the children will see that God's truth is real and reach out to experience it for themselves.

YOU

Not merely in the words you say,
Not only in your deeds confessed,
But in the most unconscious way—is Christ expressed.

Is it a beautiful smile,
A holy light upon your brow?
Oh, no! I felt His presence while you laughed—just now.
For me, 'twas not the truth you taught—
To you so clear, to me so dim—
But when you came, you brought a sense of Him.
And from your eyes He beckons me,
And from your heart His love is shed,
Till I lose sight of you and see THE CHRIST,
INSTEAD.

—Author unknown

A Learning Disciple

A leader does not have to know all the answers. "Always a learner" is the law of the disciple. We become a Christian in an instant, but discipleship takes a lifetime of learning. The leader will always be—

(a) discovering new insights into the Word;
(b) experiencing new ways God works in and through him;
(c) searching for new methods of teaching;
(d) perceiving new ways to make Bible truth applicable to the lives of children.

As he equips himself to be a better leader, he will radiate the "joy of learning" and will motivate children to "want to learn."

A Listener

A listening leader gives children opportunities to express themselves. He listens by watching expressions, by asking questions, and by allowing the children to express themselves in creative writing or art.

Listening is
the way a leader learns the needs of children;
the way he builds strong relationships;
the way he shows love and respect;
the way he builds the child's self-image;

37

the way he comes to know each child as an individual;
the way he teaches children to listen to him;
the way he learns what the children are learning.

An Enthusiastic Worker

Emerson wrote, "Enthusiasm is that all-important ingredient that more often than not makes the difference between success or failure." The word *enthusiasm* is derived from a Greek word *entheos,* which literally means "God in you."

One can be enthusiastic about children's church only if he believes children and their early experiences of worship are important, and that God wants him to serve in this ministry. No one should minister in children's church if he accepts the assignment reluctantly. This does not mean the leader will never experience difficult times. It does mean he will serve with zeal, eager interest, and commitment so he will not quit when the going gets rough.

A Dependable Doer

*Depend*ability is more desirable in a children's church worker than ability alone. The leader must be present on time (which means early) and be prepared with a well-planned children's worship service. All other qualifications combined cannot make up for a lack of dependability.

A Praying Person

There is no substitute for prayer. No amount of work can take its place. Even Satan makes light of prayerless work. Without prayer we work in human strength, but *with* prayer, God works through us to accomplish eternal results. The leader must pray for himself, the other workers, and each child. He should pray as if everything depended on God—then plan and prepare as if everything depended on him. A leader who is prepared, confident, reverent, expectant, pleasant, and sensitive to mood is one who has taken time to pray.

One Who Loves Children

Love is basic for every worker in children's church. Children can't be fooled by false caring. Love must be sincere or it is worthless. It is the ingredient that enables the leader to make each child feel that he really matters. Love helps the leader avoid comparing one child unfairly with other children. He knows and accepts their differences in maturity and background. Love makes it possible for the leader to give needed help to the disobedient, discouraged, or fearful child. He knows that many children come from homes where no one cares for or loves them. A loving leader remembers that he may be God's only "contact" person to reach children for Christ.

One Who Is Willing to Let Go and Let God

The "seeds" of the gospel fall on many types of soil. The most fertile is the heart of a child. The seeds are full of life and, in God's hands, will spring up and bring forth fruit. The good leader desires that children will become everything God wants them to be. This, however, is God's work. The leader must let God be God and not try to assume His work.

Jenny Lind was called the "Swedish Nightingale" because of her beautiful voice. Before every public appearance, she would dismiss her secretary, her maid, and her costumer. After locking the door, she would sing a note and let it fill the room. Then with her eyes closed she would look up and pray, "Master, Master, let me ring true tonight!"

When children see you, hear you, and rub shoulders with you, do you ring true? Have you meditated on God's Word until Christ's presence shines through?

These qualifications are guidelines for the children's church leader. All of them are not necessary to get started. A person who is untrained, but who loves children and wants to help, will grow with the assignment.

PART II

TAKE AIM—Plan

Football games are not won by plays, but by players who know the plays.

Planning is necessary, so all may know and understand the program and the part they play in helping children worship in ways that are pleasing to God.

TO FAIL TO PLAN
IS TO PLAN TO FAIL—

so let's plan!

CHAPTER 4

Plan for Children

Grouping

A good children's church program places the children in groups that will best meet their needs. There are no fixed rules for grouping that can be applied in all circumstances. The way children are grouped will be determined by the number and ages of the children, the adult leadership available, and the church's facilities. Consider all of these as you organize your children's church.

Plan the Grouping

Children work most effectively when they are divided according to school grade, the way it is done in Sunday School. This means that elementary age children could be grouped in a primary church (grades one and two), a middler church (grades three and four), and a junior church (grades five and six). The developmental characteristics of these three age-groups are varied enough to make it advisable to work with them separately whenever possible. (Preschool children should be cared for in their own groups. The extended session material found in the *Toddler Teacher,* the *Twos and Threes Teacher,* and the *Kindergarten Teacher* is planned for their church-time activities.)

If your church has a small number of children, limited space, or too few workers, three separate groups for children's church may not be feasible. There are several other options:

• Have two children's churches. Combine grades one, two, and three in one group, and grades four, five, and six in the other.

• Have only one group. Combine grades one through six.

• Have two children's churches. Combine middlers and juniors, and let the primary children meet separately.

• Have primary church for grades 1-3. Send grades 4-5-6 to adult worship.

• Have two churches, one for primaries and one for middlers. Send juniors to adult church.

• Combine primaries and middlers for children's worship. Send juniors to adult worship.

• Combine grades three, four, and five. Send the sixth graders to adult worship.

• Combine grades one through five. Let the sixth graders worship with the adults.

• Group the kindergartners and first graders together in one group and combine grades two, three, and four in another. Send the juniors to adult worship.

These suggestions are not exhaustive, but they should help you see various possibilities in your own situation. It is important to determine your age limits and stick to them. Don't allow a shy preschool or kindergarten child to attend children's church with an older brother or sister. Young children should be involved in extended session activities with their own age-group. Nor should older children be allowed to remain in children's church when they are past the age limit. Occasionally, a Christian seventh grader who has proven to be especially mature and good at working with children may be used as a helper.

How large should a children's church group be? A practical rule of thumb is to divide when the number of children in a group exceeds 30. Keep the group large enough to generate enthusiasm and group spirit, but always have enough workers to provide the personal attention children need from adults.

Plan the Transition into Adult Worship

Without advance planning, the time when sixth or seventh graders move into the adult worship service can be awkward and difficult. You can help make this transition easier by working with other church personnel to plan an annual service to welcome these children into adult worship. As part of the service, the pastor should give public recognition to the children and make them feel accepted.

CHAPTER 5

Plan for Workers

Neil Wiseman once told a seminary class, "The quality of your leaders is in direct proportion to the quality of your recruitment." In other words, if we want high-grade workers, our methods of enlisting them must be topnotch.

First, look critically at your own attitude toward the children's church ministry. Do you believe it is an important service? Are you challenged by the opportunity it presents? How much do you value children? These feelings will be communicated to the prospective worker you seek to recruit. Your enthusiasm, or lack of it, will show.

Next, what is the attitude of your congregation? Do pastor and people feel that working with children is a meaningful ministry? Do they see it as worthy of adult time and effort? How strongly do they affirm that children's church is a crucial part of the life and program of the church? Do they show appreciation by publicly recognizing this ministry? Do all you can to develop these attitudes in your church. Publicize the program often, then when prospective workers are approached, they will already know the importance the church places on children's church. They will be more easily recruited because people will do things they feel are important.

Help your workers know that the church feels their ministry is important by recognizing them for their efforts and praising their accomplishments. Praise and recognition are powerful motivators. One way to recognize children's workers is to hold a Commitment Service to install them in their new responsibility. Such a service will:

1. Help the congregation SEE the workers and offer their verbal support.
2. Help the congregation KNOW each leader by name.
3. Help the workers COMMIT themselves to children's church with the congregation as a witness.

Begin the service by calling the children's workers, by name, to the front of the church. Present each one with a flower to show the church's appreciation. Have the pastor describe the workers' duties and ask for their commitment. Then the pastor can lead the congregation in the following pledge of support.

> **Pastor:** We give to you part of the responsibility of training our children, knowing your work is hindered unless we all pray for you—
>
> **Congregation:** We pledge you our prayers.
>
> **Pastor:** As you commit yourselves today to teach our children and show them God's way—
>
> **Congregation:** We pledge you our prayers.
>
> **Pastor:** May you find in this task a joy and blessing that will not depart—
>
> **Congregation:** We pledge you our prayers.
>
> **Pastor:** Your influence is strong on our children. As you work in THEIR CHURCH and teach them to worship and live—
>
> **Congregation:** We pledge you our prayers.

Poor Recruitment Techniques

Before considering elements in a good recruitment program, let's look at some things to avoid:

    the quick telephone call;

    asking for a decision on the spot;

    negative approaches such as, "I don't suppose you would be interested, would you?";

    downgrading the difficulty of the work;

    rushing through the description of the job;

    the "do it for me" approach;

    desperate calls from the pulpit.

These recruiting techniques seldom produce workers who view children's church as a ministry. Usually, they succeed in staffing the children's program with people who have a "stop-gap" mentality. They are there only until someone else can be found. Many become resentful when their "temporary" job becomes permanent.

Elements in a Good Recruitment Program

Recruit with prayer. Prayerless work is powerless work. An effective children's church begins with the selection of workers. Your prayer must begin well before that.

a. Pray for yourself.

b. Consider every person you think is qualified to serve in this ministry. Ask the Holy Spirit to guide you to the ones He would have work in children's church;

c. Pray that God will speak to those you seek to recruit. Expect God to work.

Recruit in person. Do not succumb to the temptation to make a group appeal. Make the approach personal, but do not ask a person to "do it for *me.*" The prospective worker must see his service as a God-directed ministry, not as a personal favor to you.

Make an appointment to talk with the worker. Refrain from the hurried hallway conference.

Tell him honestly what the requirements of the position are and what will be expected of him. Never be guilty of trying to get an acceptance by saying there isn't much to do.

Tell the person "why" he was selected. Do you feel he has special abilities? Did God seem to direct you to him?

Let the person ask questions. Try to understand his anxiety and reluctance. Don't oversell. Gentle persuasion is a recruitment skill.

Recruit in patience. The ministry of children's church calls for spiritual leadership. Ask him to pray about the matter and give you a decision later.

Recruit for a specific period. Enlist workers for a definite period of time. One may continue longer if he wishes, but at the end of the specified length of time he may ask to be relieved of the responsibility without embarrassment or guilt. It is also important to arrange for definite "times off" during the year. Everyone needs a vacation. (See options listed in this chapter.)

Today many professional teachers experience a condition called *burnout.* Burnout occurs when an individual has given out so much he becomes tired of responsibility, resentful of his task, and apathetic toward it. This problem can occur also among volunteer children's church workers. There are many causes, but two of the main ones are (1) long periods of direct, demanding contact with children, and (2) lack of encouragement and recognition.

One strategy for strengthening children's church workers is to arrange breaks in their service. This is one reason for including vacation time in the workers' schedules.

Make an appointment to ask for the individual's decision. Allow him to volunteer; don't draft him. Accept gracefully whatever the answer is. The person knows his situation better than you do. If you get a yes, express your thanks. If you get a maybe, ask if you may come back in a week to talk further. If you get a no, express appreciation for the person's taking time to consider the position and ask him to pray for you and the ministry when God brings it to his attention.

Recruit in faith. "The harvest is great enough," Jesus remarked to His disciples, "but the reapers are few. So you must pray to the Lord of the harvest to send men out to bring it in" (Matt. 9:37-38, Phillips). It is *the Lord* who provides workers for His church.

Hudson Taylor, a pioneer in the missionary movement, once said, "God's work, done in God's way, and in God's time will never lack for God's blessing." This also applies for recruiting workers for children's church.

Plan the Staffing

The success or failure of any children's church program rests primarily with its leaders. The selection of personnel, therefore, is of utmost importance. Qualified leaders are so important that it may be wise to delay beginning your children's church rather than start with the wrong workers.

Finding the Workers

An "interest finder" will help you find hidden talent among the members of your church. It is not a panacea for all staffing problems, but it is a good place to begin. Here is a sample "interest finder."

**If you are interested in helping
in children's church,
please indicate how you will help.
Be sure to sign your name
and include your phone number.**

____ I will help every Sunday for the coming year.
____ I will help ____ Sundays each month, or ____ months a year.

_____ I will help supervise children between Sunday School and children's church in getting drinks and going to the rest rooms. (Transition Time)

_____ I will help with the music—lead singing _____, or play the piano _____.

_____ I will help make posters or equipment.

_____ I will serve as a storyteller.

_____ I will help with memory work.

_____ I will help prepare refreshments.

_____ I will do secretarial duties—mailings, bulletins, keeping records.

_____ I will help during a special series by "becoming" a Bible character and telling his story.

_____ I will help with other activities and projects when needed.

_____ I will pray regularly for the workers and children.

OTHER _____

_____

NAME _____

PHONE NUMBER _____

Adapted from *Planning Churchtime for Children,* by Betty Bowes (Kansas City: Beacon Hill Press of Kansas City, 1977).

Selecting the Staff

Once you know the interests and gifts of your congregation, you are ready to select potential workers. The children's church director is elected by the Board of Christian Life upon nomination by the pastor, chairman of the Board of Christian Life, and the director of children's ministries. Other workers are elected by the Board of Christian Life upon nomination by the children's church director, the director of children's ministries, and the pastor.

The number of workers needed will be determined by the number of children you have. The following workers are the minimum needed to begin:

Director. The director may be either a man or a woman. A husband-and-wife team may serve as codirectors. Having a man on staff in some capacity of leadership can help reduce discipline problems.

Assistant director. Having an assistant to the director guarantees that children's church goes on even when the director must be absent. The assistant director may also help with other activities.

Pianist. In addition to playing for the singing and accompanying special music, the pianist may help with other activities as needed. Where a piano or a pianist is not available, use an Autoharp, a record player, or a tape recorder to provide music.

Teachers and other helpers. One worker for every 8 to 10 children is a good ratio. Try to recruit those who are not teaching Sunday School or involved in other areas of ministry. Find persons who will make children's church a priority in their lives.

Music director (optional). If you have a children's choir program as part of the morning's activities, you will need a music director.

Staffing Suggestions

Plan No. 1. One team of workers leads children's church every Sunday FOR 11 MONTHS. They carry full responsibility for the program during this time. One month each year the children's church is dismissed so the workers can have a rest. This plan—

• Guarantees the continuity of leadership required to develop meaningful relationships between the leaders and children.

• Gives children's church workers a month of much-needed rest.

• Allows children and workers to participate in adult worship services during the vacation month.

If your church uses this plan, during the vacation month special plans must be made for the children whose parents do not regularly attend church. "Adopt-a-Child" is one workable plan. Ask adults to volunteer to "adopt" a child for the month.

Adoption includes becoming the child's friend, meeting him at his classroom when Sunday School is dismissed, allowing him to visit the rest room, and sitting with him during the service. The "adopted" child is treated just as if he were the adult's child. The child may be invited for Sunday dinner one Sunday during the month as a special treat. (Including the child's parents in the invitation might be a way to get them to attend church.)

Adults of all ages and circumstances can participate in the "adopt-a-child" plan. The only requirements are a personal experience with Christ, a love for children, and a willingness to share in the worship experience with a child. This may be the beginning of a continuing friendship between the child and the adoptive church parents.

This month of vacation for children's church workers may be featured as *CHILDREN'S MONTH*. The pastor may use one segment of the service to minister especially to the children. This is a way for him to show that he thinks children are important. His concern will help shape a positive attitude toward children's ministries in the congregation. Church members will have the opportunity to develop a sense of responsibility for the youngsters of the church, and the children will develop a sense of belonging to the group. Strongly positive feelings toward children's work will also aid future worker recruitment.

The one-month-a-year vacation is an important way to help children's church workers avoid burnout. But what about the other 11 months of the year? What can we do for them then? One answer is to provide a tape ministry. Record the morning worship service so the children's church workers can catch up on what happened in the service they missed.

Plan No. 2. Two teams of workers are enlisted for children's church—one for the regular services and one for the missionary emphasis. This plan combines children's church and the children's mission education program. Twelve times a year the mission education team relieves the regular children's church team. This plan—

- Is flexible. The missionary education team can present their part of the program for three consecutive Sundays each quarter, 12 Sundays in the summer, or one Sunday a month.
- Emphasizes world evangelization. Children may sense God's call and respond to it during their elementary years.
- Is resourced by the Children's Mission Study Kit and the missionary reading books.
- Requires coordination between the two teams.
- Gives the regular workers needed rest. The director or assistant director in the regular team should attend children's church during the missionary emphasis. This insures that there will be at least one adult present every Sunday whom the children know well. These leaders, however, are not responsible for the program on those Sundays.

Plan No. 3. Two teams of workers alternate in presenting the units of study. One team teaches one unit, the second team teaches the next unit. Both teams are under one director. This plan—

- Allows extended preparation time for the workers.
- Allows workers more "time off" so they come to the sessions more refreshed.
- Requires close coordination between the teams. Having both teams coordinated by one director gives the children a person with whom to identify. However, this leader should have at least one month's vacation every year.
- Provides the children with a greater number of Christian adult models.
- Requires each team to be responsible for the full program only one-half of the time.
- Allows workers in the two teams to be more involved in the life of the adult congregation.

Plan No. 4. One director, or a set of codirectors, has complete responsibility for children's church with the help of a rotating staff. This plan—

- Involves adults who cannot work every week in children's church.
- Provides the continuity of leadership that is important to children.
- Utilizes dependable high school age young people as helpers. It is important for teens to worship with their peers in adult services some of the time. They may alternate their attendance between children's church and adult church every month or every unit of study. Make sure that teen helpers understand their duties and carry them out responsibly.

Plan No. 5. One team of workers conducts children's church only through the school months. During the summer months everyone attends the regular worship services. This plan—

- Gives workers two to three months of vacation from their responsibilities. Arrangements must be made for the children from nonchurch families who will be attending adult worship during the summer months. (See Plan No. 1.)
- Contributes to building relationships between the children and the workers since they have only one group of workers for the year.

Plan 5 is recommended only as a last resort. Special care must be taken to avoid creating in the children the feeling that they are being abandoned in the summer.

Training Workers

Is the wisest way to find leadership for children's church to look for "ready-made" leaders or to look for leaders who can be "made ready"? If you have ready-made leaders, use them! If not, make them ready through *training.*

Children learn more from the leader's example than from anything he may say. When selecting a children's church leader, consider what he is more than what he can do. However, it is unfair both to the worker and to the children to recruit an inexperienced worker and leave him to his own devices. As an anonymous writer put it, "God is not served by incompetence."

Willingness to learn is as important as present knowledge or past experience. There should be a place in children's church for the person who loves God, loves children, is cooperative, and *is willing to learn.*

Consider these training possibilities that are available for children's church workers.

- A *Continuing Lay Training* course using this book as the text is an excellent beginning. The course may be completed in a group as a class or individually in a home study program.
- District Christian Life and Sunday School Conventions often include special workshops for children's workers. Urge children's church workers to attend.
- Read books and magazines. The front sections of the Sunday School teachers' manuals often have instructive material. *Resource* magazine has many articles to help those working in children's church.
- The special age-group CLT texts are a must for those who wish to learn how to work with children.
- Observe a good Sunday School teacher in action.
- Set up a plan of in-service training. The trainee may become an assistant, working under the leadership of an experienced leader. He may start by watching, advance to helping, and then move to taking charge now and then. This enables the new worker to gain experience without carrying the full responsibility at the beginning of his service. As his confidence is established, he may be given additional responsibilities.
- Study the instructional materials prepared for children's

church. One user wrote, "Your *Leader's Guide* is wonderfully detailed, which is just what new workers need to teach them how to do the job right. The step-by-step directions for the morning schedule have eliminated many insecurities for our new workers!"

CHAPTER 6

Plan the Environment

A medical doctor once said that he could cure no one. He simply put a person in the very best physical environment he could so that the Great Physician could do His work.

Children's church leaders can't make any child know God. But they can create an environment in which God can reveal himself to the child.

The development of children is determined largely by the "climate" in which they live. In the context of children's church, "climate" refers to (1) the physical surroundings, (2) the social atmosphere, (3) and the emotional tone. Leaders must always be aware of the fact that the learning environment is constantly sending messages to the child.

Physical Surroundings

The room is the most obvious part of the learning environment. It should be far enough away from the adult sanctuary so that neither adults nor children disturb each other. It should be large enough so there is space to arrange chairs in rows for a worship service, yet flexible enough to allow for dramatization and small-group activities. If you share a room with another ministry (Sunday School, Caravan, etc.), work together on a plan that meets the needs of both.

Look critically at your room. How does it make you feel? Does it make you want to enter? What in the room is beautiful? Does it have a focal point that leads to worship? Are there activity centers that beckon the child to enter? Does the room say, "Come on in! Exciting things are going on here!" Does it say, "God is in this place"?

Equipping your room with "church" furnishings can aid worship. Stained-glass windows made from multicolored self-adhesive paper (such as Con-Tact) will make the room look more like a sanctuary. A child-sized pulpit and altar is also appropriate. They can be made from scrap materials and stained or painted. Even if you have only a small room, a low platform adds to the churchlike atmosphere. Small offering plates, a chalkboard, bulletin board, easel, and audiovisual equipment should also be on hand. Plants and flowers are a beautiful addition and remind the children of the work of our Creator.

One question that should always be kept in mind is, "Can everyone see what is going on?"

Changing the appearance and arrangement of the room adds interest and helps to eliminate an "in-the-rut" feeling. Chairs placed in rows focus attention in one place. Arranged in a semicircle they promote conversation and give a more relaxed atmosphere.

A comfortable environment aids worship. Children usually become restless in a room that is too warm or too cold. Be sure the lighting and ventilation are adequate. Be sensitive to your children's church's physical environment. For example, if your windows are small, brighten up the room with stained-glass window murals.

Use good equipment and insist that the room be clean and as attractive as possible. Indirectly, this teaches the children that God's work deserves the best.

Social Atmosphere

A child's learning is greatly influenced by the way he feels toward the group. A good social "climate" is created when the children care about one another.

Often there is at least one child who is not well accepted by the rest of the group. Leaders in children's church must spot those rejected or those loosely involved—the isolated ones. They need to get to know those children and try to analyze *why* the rejection is there.

One Sunday morning after our children's church moved from the transitional/variety time area to the worship room, Mark, a shy child, was not singing. The seats next to him were vacant. No one wanted to sit by him. Of course, he wasn't singing! He felt the sting of rejection by his peers.

In such situations, the leader must be certain *he* accepts the child. His attitude, good or bad, will be catching. Once he is sure of his position, the leader can plan to help the other children appreciate the isolated child. This can be done by helping the group take the other child's role, and see things through his eyes. DO THIS ONLY WHEN THE ISOLATED CHILD IS NOT PRESENT. Children who feel rejected by their peers in the church may feel rejected by God. A healthy social atmosphere is necessary for every child to receive the greatest benefit from his children's church experience.

In any group, children have the right to expect the leader to establish a social climate where unkind behavior is unacceptable.

Emotional Tone

Emotional tone is closely related to the social atmosphere. A good emotional tone is one in which there is love, appreciation, and respect for each child. Each individual feels he is important, loved by God, and a person of worth and dignity.

One way to help a child feel a sense of worth is to greet him by name when he arrives. If possible, visit with the child before a worker helps him find an activity.

A child questions his value when he is made fun of, embarrassed, or ignored. On the other hand, he will glow when he is accepted, when his ideas are used, and when he is treated with respect. Learning is hampered severely when children feel threatened emotionally or physically. Their attention and energies are directed toward dealing with feelings of fear and self-doubt rather than toward the learning activities.

As leader, you *must* be "in charge" if the emotional tone is conducive to worship. Dr. Haim G. Ginott, in his book *Teacher and Child,* says, "I have come to a frightening conclusion. I am the decisive element in the classroom. It is my personal approach that creates the climate. It is my daily mood that makes the weather." There is no way for the leader to get off the hook when it comes to placing responsibility for the "climate" in children's church.

The single most important factor in the environment for children's church is the adult staff. Their relationships with Christ and attitudes toward themselves, the children, and their ministry will be readily observed by the children. These must be worthy of copying.

Attitudes are conveyed in many ways. Verbal messages —what we say about the way we feel—are the most easily recognized. But nonverbal attitude communication is equally important. Facial expressions, tone of voice, silence, eye contact—all influence emotional tone. How one dresses may not seem to be of great importance, but it is one of the aspects to which children respond. Touch is another important means of nonverbal communication with children. However, it must be used with care. While most children need it, some are not ready to accept it. Facial expressions are a very obvious means of communication to a child. You may say, "I'm not angry with you," but if you wear a scowl, the child will believe the scowl, not the words. If you smile warmly at a newcomer, he will feel you like him, even though you haven't said so. The tone of your voice, and even your silence, can communicate feelings: anger, love, rejection, or acceptance.

Children are skillful in interpreting nonverbal communication. It is the way they learned how to talk. Kind words will not mask an unhealthy attitude. In working with children, the basic question is, "Do we really care?" The answer must be an unqualified Yes! We have access to love that persists beyond our own strength, because it comes from God. Our task is to let children know God loves them. The environment we provide in children's church will either add to or detract from that message.

Plan the Administration

Finance

A children's church program need not be expensive. However, definite plans for financing it should be made before this ministry is launched.

The budget is recommended by the Board of Christian Life and approved by the church board. The amount of money needed depends on the number of children involved. The major cost will be for supplies—paper, pencils, glue, crayons, etc. The first year money will be needed for start-up costs. Furnishings and other items should be viewed as an investment in children.

The children's church program may become self-supporting if children are taught to give systematically. Using tithe envelopes gives the boys and girls a sense of personal pride in their giving. They will also be encouraged to give regularly if they see the adult workers giving their tithes and offering.

Tithes and offerings collected in children's church are turned in to the church treasurer. The children's church director keeps a record of this money, along with the records of money expended. This information is included in his monthly report to the director of children's ministries, who will then report it to the Board of Christian Life.

Publicity

A short time before you start children's church, send an information letter to every parent. Describe the program, its goals, what is expected of the children, and ways the church and home can work together. Parents must be informed if you expect their cooperation.

Keep the whole church aware of the children's church program through interesting items in the church bulletin and/or newsletter. This is extremely important. If possible, include an article about children's church at least once a month. List the names of children who have won special honors for perfect attendance and memory work. This gives children needed recognition and provides occasions for the parents to experience justified pride in their children's accomplishments. Such information is also important to insure financial and prayer support from the congregation.

Don't forget to *let the children know* what is happening. Make announcements exciting. To create interest in starting children's worship, one church had a boy act out the part of a well-known cartoon character. Wearing a costume of the character left over from Halloween, he went to each class and asked where children's church would be held so he could attend. Cartoons were put in the weekly newsletter and used on posters with such captions as "Happiness is a cookie before church begins"; "Of course, I'm taking my Bible and blanket to children's church." Keep your children informed.

Resources

What resources are available? This question is often asked in children's church workshops. Here is a list of some. Check your current publishing house catalog for a complete list.

Preschool Curriculum

Material for preschool extended sessions is printed in the *Toddler Teacher, Twos and Threes Teacher,* and *Kindergarten Teacher.*

Elementary Curriculum

For elementary age children, the following items are available:

Leading Children in Worship, Volumes 1, 2, and 3, support the quarterly themes of your Sunday School lessons.

52 Sundays of Worship for Children, book one and book two, offer programs emphasizing spiritual growth. The index makes it easy to pick a unit with a theme you need at a special time.

Children's Mission Study Kit. Historically, missions has been an integral part of the Church of the Nazarene. Each assembly year a kit with 12 children's studies, complete with visuals and activities, examines one big mission idea: culture, the missionary, mission support system, the Bible and mission, and Christian responsibility. These studies are designed to be informative as well as inspirational. The format allows them to be used easily in the children's church setting. A set of children's missionary reading books is available to reinforce the studies in the kit.

Children's Church Packets. These packets contain a leader's guide and visuals for one unit of study. They are undated and written on timely subjects. They may be used as elective children's church curriculum.

Evangelistic Helps

Really Living is a colorful illustrated booklet which explains the plan of salvation to girls and boys. The *Really Living Lead-*

er's Guide tells leaders how to use the *Really Living* booklet. A *Really Living Poster Set* is also available. It is an enlarged version (17″ x 24″) of *Really Living* for large group use.

Living . . . as a Christian is a booklet of 16 devotions to help children who have recently accepted Christ become established in their faith.

Bible Memorization

Learning Bible verses can be an important part of the children's church program. Children's Ministries has developed a complete *Bible Memorization Program* for children. The *Leader's Guide* contains vital information on the value of Bible memorization and the responsibilities of directors and sponsors in organizing and carrying out this program. The guide also contains the verses for each age-group, games and activities for helping children understand and memorize scripture, and a description of the incentive plan.

Pupil's books are available for kindergartners through juniors. They explain, on the child's level, the importance of scripture memorization, along with tips for memorizing and the rules for receiving awards.

Each book contains the verses to be learned. Verses are printed in both the King James and the *New International Version.* A space is provided for the child to check off each passage when it is memorized.

A number of awards are offered to motivate children and recognize their achievement. Certificates, seals, a ribbon, and a trophy are available.

Songbooks

Music is an important part of worship. The following songbooks are graded for use with children.

Songs of God and Me. These singable songs for primaries have been selected to support the themes of Aldersgate curriculum. This book also contains some arrangements suitable for children's choir.

Sing! Songs for juniors. This songbook for juniors has 95 enjoyable, singable songs.

Joyfully Sing! Use with middlers and juniors.

Something to Sing About, by Suzanne H. Clason, is a versatile collection of songs for children. They are practical for group singing and well suited for younger choirs.

Children's Praises contains songs and hymns for boys and girls of all ages. It has been a standard songbook for many years.

Other Helpful Books and Supplies

Egermeier's Bible Story Book

When You Need a Story, by Elizabeth Jones, is a good source for extra stories.

Puppets Go to Church, by Wilma and Earl Perry, considers the place of puppets in the church's ministry. It is a useful training book that also includes puppet scripts.

The Puppet Ministry, by Jim Christy, deals with the purpose, philosophy, principles, methods, and performance of puppets in church. It contains 18 puppet scripts.

Let's Teach with Bible Games, by Donna Fillmore, gives plans for many games that can be used in children's church. Games are popular with boys and girls. Use them to help make your message come alive for the children.

You will also need supplies for doing the creative activities in children's church. Some you will use almost every Sunday are crayons, scissors, felt-tipped markers, paste, paper, pencils, chalk, and yarn.

Simple costumes are valuable for use in creative drama. A box of old sheets, strips of material, and old clothing will add much to dramatic experiences.

Consult your current publishing house catalog for new resources that are available.

Program

Before the first children's church service is held, all workers should meet and plan the year's calendar. *Leading Children in Worship* simplifies this task. Each volume contains a full year's program, but probably you will not use all of the sessions because of special services, mission education, and times when you take the children to be a part of regular church worship.

SPECIAL NOTE: Each of the three volumes supports the themes of the Sunday School lessons for a specific curriculum year. Check with your director of children's ministries to make sure you use the correct volume.

When arranging the calendar, plan for the children to worship with the adults on the Sunday after a unit of study has been completed. Note also the Sundays when special services are scheduled for the entire church. Plan to dismiss children's church when these services would be interesting to the children, such as a missionary service. And of course you will have to plan around such events as the Christmas program, the VBS program, Children's Sunday, and so on.

Once you have the annual calendar established, keep communication channels open among workers with monthly or quarterly staff meetings.

At these meetings deal with problems that may arise, and plan specific units of study. Pray for the needs of the children's church.

Every Sunday's session should be planned well in advance. Each session plan in *Leading Children in Worship* has a specific objective that should be accomplished. The music, story, message, and activities should lead to and support that objective. Be sure you include children in the services (special music, ushers, and worship leaders). This may be more work than doing everything yourself, but participation is an important way children learn.

68

Attending adult worship is such an important part of the children's church program that it needs further consideration. Here are three ways that are commonly used.

1. Children attend adult worship on the Sunday after each unit of study has been completed. From the standpoint of the teaching/learning process, this is the best method because it does not disrupt a series of lessons. It also establishes a regular pattern that is easy to remember.

2. Children attend adult worship one Sunday each quarter and during special services.

3. Children attend adult worship one Sunday each month, usually the same Sunday.

Be sure to include the pastor in your planning. Let him know when the children will attend adult worship. Suggest that he consider including features of special interest to the children: (1) singing a hymn the children know; (2) telling a story or giving an object lesson; (3) giving each child an activity sheet related to the sermon. These activity sheets are a good way for the pastor to find out what the children learn in the adult service.

Another effective way to help keep the children interested during the adult worship is to give assignments to the different age-groups. For example, ask one group to listen to all the music and report in children's church next Sunday which song they liked best. Ask another group to share something they learned from the sermon.

When the children attend adult worship, make sure each one knows where he is to sit and with whom. Those whose parents are present may sit with them. Children whose parents do not attend church may be assigned to sit with "adoptive" parents. Since one goal of having the children attend adult worship is to help them feel they are part of the larger church family, it is usually better not to have the children's church sit together as a group. An exception to this is if the children are to be present for only part of the adult service and then go to their own room.

Before taking the children to the sanctuary, be sure everyone has visited the rest room and has had a snack and a drink.

PART III

SHOOT—Act

(On Sunday Morning)

Builder

A builder builded a temple;
  He wrought with care and skill.
Pillars and groins and arches
  Were fashioned to meet his will;
And men said when they saw its beauty;
  "It shall never know decay.
Great is thy skill, O Builder,
  Thy fame shall endure for aye."

A teacher builded a temple;
  She wrought with skill and care;
Forming each pillar with patience,
  Laying each stone with prayer.
None saw the unceasing effort;
  None knew of the marvelous plan;
For the temple the teacher builded
  Was unseen by the eyes of man.

Gone is the builder's temple;
  Crumbled into the dust,
Pillars and groins and arches
  Food for consuming rust;
But the temple the teacher builded
  Shall endure while the ages roll;
For that beautiful, unseen temple
  Was a child's immortal soul.

—Author unknown

CHAPTER 8

Sunday Morning Options

All of the work up to this point has been directed at preparing for Sunday morning. However, the best plans, the greatest staff, and the finest facilities are only good intentions unless they are brought together with the help of the Holy Spirit.

One of the most critical factors in the success or failure of a children's church program is scheduling. Below are four options that have worked well in different churches. No single plan will work for everyone, everywhere. The best one for you will be the one *you adapt* to fit your needs.

The Three-part Service

This plan has three basic components, with approximately the same amount of time devoted to each part.

1. Between Sunday School and Worship Time
2. Worship Time
3. Life Response

One difficult aspect of the Sunday morning schedule is the time between Sunday School and children's church. This is a time of transition that allows the children to move and get rid of the "built-in wiggles." It also prepares them for worship. Mass movement in the halls is often chaotic. It can be orderly, however, if the children are supervised properly. An adult helper can meet each class at its classroom door and walk with the children to the worship area.

During the time between Sunday School and children's church the children should get drinks and use the rest room. Many children come to church without breakfast. Transition time provides an opportunity for simple refreshments. Avoid foods with a high sugar content. This can make some children overactive. Use wholesome, nutritious snacks such as grape, apple, or orange juice and soda or graham crackers. Be sure to check on possible allergies.

Transition time is an important part of children's church. It sets the tone for the service to follow. The atmosphere should be inviting. Provide a variety of activities from which the children may choose. These should introduce them to the theme of the worship time or review past sessions.

The three *Leading Children in Worship* volumes contain directions for transition activities. They may include music, games, crafts, reading, art, or just talking about the children's week.

Worship follows the transition period. Since the objectives of children's church include "To provide worship experiences that will deepen the child's Christian life," the most important part of the morning is worship. At this time the children's thoughts are directed toward God.

Children must learn how to worship. Even adults are often uncertain about what worship is and how one worships. You must have a clear understanding of the meaning of worship before you try to teach children. Worship is both an attitude and an act. It is an attitude of reverence and adoration. As an act it involves listening and obeying. Children learn much more from your attitudes and actions in worship than from all the words they hear about worship.

Worship time should include music, prayer, scripture, offering, and the Bible message.

Music can awaken reverence, bring joy, and inspire devotion. Choose the songs carefully for their message and musical quality. Singing is a worship experience in which everyone can participate. Even children who are too timid to pray aloud will often sing with a group.

Your children may enjoy learning a "hymn of the month." Ask your church's song leader to have the congregation sing the song of the month when the children attend adult worship.

Prayer is a vital part of worship. Children should be taught to use ordinary language when they pray. Encourage communication with God as a natural part of the Christian life.

God's Word should be the central focus of worship. Guide the children to love and respect the Bible. Teach them how to apply Scripture to their lives.

When you refer to a particular Bible passage, give the reference and wait until each child has found the place in his Bible. Workers should assist those who have difficulty finding it. Patience is the key in helping children use their Bibles. Having children use their Bibles in children's church teaches them valuable skills and emphasizes that these stories are true because they are in the Bible. They are about real people and real events.

The offering should be an important part of worship. Giving makes the child aware of his responsibility to the church and helps him feel a part of the work of God.

The message must be relevant to the children's experience, something they can use. While some methods are naturally entertaining, teaching is the purpose of the message. Children should remember that the puppet taught them that the Bible says it is wrong to steal, rather than just remember how funny the puppet was.

In all segments of children's church, but especially in the message, mere human effort is not enough. The Holy Spirit must apply the truth to the children's hearts. Handle Bible truths accurately.

No matter how thrilling the material seemed to the writers and editors, unless you take the time to make the message live, it will remain as flat as the paper on which it was printed.

The children's church hour is not complete until the children have had opportunities to apply the truth to their lives and respond to it. Remember, worship also includes acting upon what one has learned. That is why the third portion of the three-part service is called "Life Response." It comes at the end of the session when children need to be active.

The purpose of "Life Response" is to reinforce the message by letting the children respond in some concrete way. As you plan the service, keep this question in mind: "What do I want the children to DO because of this message?" The curriculum provides a variety of activities that let children respond to the message. For example, if your morning theme has been prayer, the children could make a prayer booklet containing a list of prayer requests and space to write in the answers.

The Extended Session

This plan is a continuation of the Sunday School lesson theme through the church hour. The same purposes apply for both Sunday School and church time. This allows a larger block of time to be given to a lesson than either Sunday School or children's church alone can provide. Many churches use the extended session plan for preschool children, but it may also be used with older groups.

Ideally, when the extended session plan is used, the persons who have charge of Sunday School should remain with the children and conduct the extended session. Young children learn better when there is a continuity of workers. However, if it is impossible to find adults who will devote their entire Sunday morning to working with children, a second set of workers may take over during the break between Sunday School and church time.

The extended session plan requires the Sunday School and church time workers to coordinate their efforts and share one lesson plan for the entire Sunday morning period. When the second set of workers slips into the room, they can quietly take over and continue the learning activity in which the children are engaged.

Material planned for use in preschool extended sessions is included in *Twos and Threes Teaches* and *Kindergarten Teacher.*

Since the end of the extended session must coincide with the close of the adult service, be prepared with activities the children *especially enjoy* for those times when the adult service runs longer than usual. It is important to keep the children happily involved or some will become apprehensive because their parents are delayed.

The Mini-adult Service

This plan patterns the church time for children after the adult worship service. It is distinguished from the adult service in that it uses materials written on the child's level, and methods that involve the children. However, the children do not move to learning centers or tables.

In planning for the service, select the theme, decide on the methods of presentation, assign the different segments of the service to workers, and arrange your "Order of Service." Give a copy of the plan to every worker. This will help to keep the service moving smoothly from one segment to another. Lag time between the different parts of the service can foster discipline problems.

Here is a suggested "Order of Service":
> Call to Worship
> Singing
> Prayer Song
> Moments of Prayer
> Scripture Memory Time
> Offering
> Music
> Bible Story
> Special Music
> Life-related Story
> Song
> Benediction
> (Optional-Review Games)

The Divided Service

If this plan is used, the children attend part of the adult worship service, usually during the congregational singing, prayer time, and special music, and a short message prepared especially for them. At a predetermined point, the children are dismissed to go quietly to their own service. The children should understand that they are leaving because the pastor will be preaching to the adults. He will use concepts and language that will be hard for them to understand. They are not leaving because the rest of the service is uninteresting.

The benefits of this plan include helping the children to feel a part of the larger church family, exposing them to adult modes of worship, making the congregation aware of the need for children's worship, and helping the children identify more closely with the pastor.

There are some drawbacks to the plan. Many times music *for children* is omitted. The break in the service when the children leave may be disruptive. Weaknesses such as these can be eliminated if the pastor and the children's church workers plan together. They need to coordinate the message with the activities that follow.

The Modular Plan

This plan combines the time for Sunday School and the church hour into one block. The period is divided into equal, or nearly equal, time modules. Each module has a different leader. The children may move from leader to leader, or the leaders may move from group to group.

The modular plan is unusually flexible and is easily adapted to various local situations. It is also easy to include special emphases in the schedule, such as quizzing, Bible memorization, puppetry, and program practice.

A three-module plan for 2½ hours might be organized like this:

	Primary	*Middler*	*Junior*
9:30-10:15	Worship	Music and Memorization	Activity
10:20-11:05	Activity	Worship	Music and Memorization
11:10-12:00	Music and Memorization	Activity	Worship

In this schedule, two modules contain 45 minutes each and the third has 50 minutes. Five minutes have been allowed for the children or leaders to move from one module to the next. Nine teachers would be required since all three groups are involved in a different activity at the same time. Additional workers, such as pianists and lead teachers, would also be needed.

If 2½ hours are not available, adjust the schedule by shortening the time the children spend in each module. If there are fewer children so you do not need three groups, put grades 1-3 together and grades 4-6 together. The plan may also be expanded into a four- or five-module schedule by adding modules. Two possibilities are (1) Bible Lesson, and (2) Christian Living. If this is done, adjust the time for the modules as necessary, leaving five minutes between each one for moving, and recruit additional teachers.

The modular plan is workable in many situations, but it is not a cure-all. Lack of space is often the reason for adopting this kind of schedule. This may mean the worship area is less than ideal. Regardless of what the room is like, make it as attractive and as worshipful as possible.

Time coordination is essential if the modular plan is to work. Rooms must be cleared with as little delay as possible. This makes it difficult to deal with children who respond when an invitation is given, but the problem is not insurmountable. When an invitation is planned, the time and arrangement of the modules can be adjusted. If the invitation is spontaneous, the children who respond can be moved to another room for counseling and prayer.

Time loss tends to occur each time the children or leaders move. It is essential that the teacher begin as soon as the children arrive. If it is not possible to prepare the room before the children arrive, the teacher may have teaching materials ready in a large box.

Some teachers find it difficult to adjust to teaching only a portion of the materials. The idea of sharing in the children's learning experiences, especially when the other teachers cannot be seen, must be developed. The attitude of "my class" must be discouraged in favor of "our children." This is a hard-to-handle problem for some teachers who have always had full responsibility for a group.

The success of any children's church schedule depends upon the leaders, a well-planned organization, and a service prepared to interest the children and meet their needs. The variables among churches are so many it is not feasible to say, "This is THE plan. Use it." Carefully study the five plans above, then tailor your own plan for a children's church that ministers effectively to the children in your group.

PART IV

PRACTICE—Make It Better

Immortal Words

An idea placed on parchment may be blotted
    out with dust,
Engraved in granite, may wear away,
In iron, erode with rust;
In marble, it may be covered with moss,
Or the elements melt it away;
But thoughts implanted in the heart of a child
Will never meet decay.
For the heart of a child
Is an immortal soul,
Which will live forever
While eternity may roll.
If you would seek for permanence
That nothing can destroy,
Then write your words of wisdom
On the heart of a girl or boy.

—Helen L. Morse

CHAPTER 9

Music Is for Children

Music Is for Everyone— but It Is Especially for Children!

God created music.

He also made us able to hear, enjoy, and respond to the music He created.

By creating people in His image, He makes us able to create music too. When He comes into our lives, He brings His creativity with Him.

Music is a tool to communicate spiritual truths. It can be a vital part of children's church.

Music Is Everywhere

Music is often in the background as we do housework, eat dinner, shop, ride, and work. Advertising experts recognize the value of music to keep their products in the minds of the people. Have you ever wished you "were an Oscar Mayer weiner"? Or have you ever realized that "nobody, nobody can do it like

McDonalds can" because they "do it all for you"? The experts know that an idea coupled with a singable tune will stick. These tunes remain in the subconscious mind and surface at the appropriate moment.

Music can, however, do more than sell a product. In children's church, good music can set a mood, create an atmosphere for worship or prayer, teach scripture, help children learn about themselves, or expand a lesson point. Well-chosen, well-led music can do all these things and more.

Music Can Serve Many Purposes

Music draws a group together. Children come to children's church from a wide variety of backgrounds. As they sing together, they begin to think together.

Music is an educational tool, not just a time filler. Learning occurs on three levels:

a. Intellectual, as music increases retention and helps children think about what they are singing;

b. Emotional, as they sense the mood of the song;

c. Physical, as they go through the motions of action songs.

Music involves the entire person with its message. How many times have you been sustained in a time of testing by a Christian song?

Music is a vital part of worship. It can draw the child into a meaningful, happy expression of praise. It can turn the child's thoughts toward God. It can bring conviction.

Music can serve as a bridge from one activity to another. It can even be used to sing instructions, especially for the preschoolers.

Music, especially musicals, train children for singing in a church choir. Musicals also attract unchurched parents. When their children are performing, many parents will attend.

Music can be an evangelistic tool at home. As children sing the songs they have learned, they share the gospel with the rest of their family.

Music Is for Participation

Musical participation is at a low point in our culture. Many homes have little wholesome musical exposure. Children are more accustomed to being entertained than being actively involved. Television has tended to encourage children to be passive observers instead of active participants.

Yet children learn best when they are actively involved. What better way is there to encourage participation than through music? As they sing, the concepts you are teaching become a part of them. However, to be most effective, music must be chosen carefully for a specific instructional purpose, not just to fill time.

Help children learn not only the words and music of songs but also their meaning. Here are some ideas to use.
1. Have the children illustrate the song with a rebus, a montage, or a mural.
2. Assign groups to listen to the song and see if they hear particular items.
3. Ask children what feelings were expressed in the music.
4. Let the children tell how the music makes them feel and why.
5. Compare the song with Scripture.

Every child is a potential singer. However, if a child does not sing, don't create anxiety for him by pointing it out. Perhaps the child is just trying to learn the song by listening. He will sing with the others when he is ready. Sometimes, however, a little encouragement may be needed to clear away an inhibition.

Music Should Be Relevant

Choose your music carefully and purposefully. Ask yourself,

"Will this music draw the children closer to God and help them learn about His Word?" Not all music is suitable for children's church. Here are some standards to help you evaluate the lyrics of a song:

(1) The idea should be expressed in words the children can understand. This enables them to sing with meaning and to relate the music to their lives. Ask, "What does the song say to those who will sing it?" Always explain any new or difficult words. Children like to learn some new words, but avoid songs that have too many.

(2) The lyrics should express right ideas about God, Jesus, and the Christian way of life. The ideas must be doctrinally sound.

(3) The ideas should be expressed concretely. Children often misunderstand symbolism. Any symbolic language that cannot be easily explained to the literally minded child should be avoided.

(4) The lyrics should be worthy of being sung. Many songs written for children are cheap jingles. They are not worthy of our great faith. Pack *substance* into your songs.

(5) The ideas in the song should be related to the purpose of the session. They should help you accomplish your objectives.

Music Should Be Singable

The words of a song are important, but the music is also important. The melody of the song should be easy to sing, so children will learn the song quickly and remember it. Select songs with the following musical characteristics.

(1) The music should fit the mood of the words. For example, a prayer song should be quieting and reverent, not sung to a lively march tune.

(2) The melody should have a strong rhythm—a flow of musical phrases that the singer can feel.

(3) The harmony should be simple and should never obscure the melody. In playing music for preschool children, the instrumentalists should seldom play more than the melody. Instrumental harmony may be added to kindergarten music after the children have learned a song.

(4) The vocal range of the song should be comfortable for children. Children sing most easily in an octave ranging from middle C to C above middle C. Avoid music with wide swings in the melody. A melody should lead easily up to and down from high notes.

Introducing New Music

Try to introduce new music in ways that will be interesting and enjoyable for your children. Here are some ideas:

(1) Read the words aloud. Talk about the song. Ask questions and discuss the new music.

(2) Teach the last line first, then add lines until the song is completely memorized.

(3) Study pictures that interpret the words.

(4) Act out the song.

(5) Locate the concept behind the song. Study the background scripture.

(6) Clap the rhythm before singing the notes.

(7) Make flash cards with the song's words.

(8) Make or purchase song visuals.

(9) Play games to learn the words. Cover parts of the song on your chart and let the children sing the hidden parts without the words. Continue hiding additional words until children can sing the song from memory.

(10) Use puppets to teach the song.

Remember, repetition is the key to memorization. However, do not spend too much time on a new song. Come back to it later. If a song fails, leave it and try it another time. If it still fails, forget it. Move swiftly from one song to another and keep the children involved.

Your own attitude toward music is contagious. Yawn, and your singers will yawn too. Mumble your words, and the children will mumble. Barely sing, and you will find it hard to hear the children. But smile and enjoy the song, and everyone else will brighten up too.

10

The Bible—Use It

One of the primary goals of children's church is to help children develop a love for God's Word. To do this effectively, you must know the Bible well yourself. Only then will you be able to share your knowledge with the children and help them learn to use the Bible in their own lives.

The Bible is the most timely book ever written; but more than that, it is the Word of God! Your attitude, love, and respect for the Bible will be a model for the children. Share with them how God is using His Word to direct and help you. This will help them feel that the Bible is a living Book and will motivate them to want to learn to use it.

Developing Basic Bible Skills

Make an effort in every session to give your children an opportunity to get to know the Bible better. See that each child has his own Bible. If some do not, perhaps the church could provide one. If this is done, be sure to purchase Bibles with print suitable for young readers.

Introduce the children to the contents page of their Bibles. This will list all of the books in order. Challenge them to memorize the books of the Bible. Singing them to a familiar tune is one effective way to do this. Other techniques are given in the children's church curriculum.

Bible Memorization

Ever stop to take note
  How our girls and our boys
Tread along in the path we have led them.
How their spiritual stature
  and physical form
Bear the marks of the food we have fed them.
                              —Roy E. McCaleb

In our changing world we feel the need for something that never changes, something to which we can cling. Children are also caught in the whirl of this swiftly moving age. They too need something constant. What is more sure than the Word of God?

For God's Word to be of greatest benefit, children need to have it hidden in their heart. When a need arises, there is not always time or opportunity to seek the help of an older Christian or to search God's Word for guidance. If the child has memorized a passage from God's Word, the Spirit may bring it to mind just when he needs it most.

Some children feel they cannot learn Bible verses. Others dislike all memorizing. Most adult workers believe that Bible memorization is important, but many don't know how to make it interesting. To be effective, teach Bible verses "three dimensionally."

I. What does the verse SAY?
   a. Visualize the verse using word cards, drawings, or pictures.
   b. Encourage children to read the verse from the Bible.
   c. Allow time for children to read the verse and say it.

    d. Let the children write the verse.

    e. Play a game with the verse. This provides effective motivation to memorize it.

II. What does the verse MEAN?

    a. Explain the verse carefully word by word, phrase by phrase.

    b. Ask children to write or tell, in their own words, what the verse means.

    c. Discuss the verse.

    d. Have the children draw pictures to show what the verse means.

III. How can I APPLY the verse?

    a. Share your experiences in applying Scripture.

    b. Show how the verse applies to the children's lives.

    c. Plan an activity so the children can use what they have learned, preferably during the next week.

Use games and exercises to make memorization easier, challenging, and fun. Activities for Bible memorization are given in the children's church curriculum. Here are some sample ideas.

1. Mouse House. Put wood-grain adhesive paper on the bottom (the flap) of a lunch-sized paper bag. In the center, about half an inch up from the edge, cut a round hole large enough to push a mouse finger puppet through.

The mouse puppet can teach a memory verse by asking the children to "repeat after me" the phrases of a verse. A second technique is to have the mouse make deliberate mistakes and let the children correct the mouse's misquotation. As they do this, they impress the correct words in their own minds.

2. Put strips of felt on cards and place the cards on a flannel board. Scramble them and let one or two children arrange the verse in order.

3. Write the verse on a chalkboard. Have the children read the verse. Erase a word or phrase and let the children repeat the verse. Continue erasing words and saying the verse until children have memorized it.

4. Quote the verse, leaving out certain words. Ask volunteers to tell what word you left out.

5. Use the verse as a response to a life situation. For instance:

> Teacher: "When it is dark at night . . ."
> Class: "I will trust and not be afraid."

6. For longer passages, read the verses responsively. Girls may read one verse, boys another. Or assign parts. Review is essential for retaining material that has been memorized. However, review is boring unless it is varied, to the point, and fun. Using the ideas above can help make scripture review time a highlight of children's church.

Recognize Achievement

Bible memorization is hard work. The true rewards of knowing scripture "by heart" are realized in times of special need, but it is important to provide children with "intermediate" rewards. Recognizing their achievements motivates them to continue learning scripture until they discover the true value for themselves.

In the *Bible Memorization Program* a variety of awards are available. Write to your publishing house for a flyer describing this program. If you use this program in children's church, print in your church newsletter the names of the children who have completed portions of the program.

Other ideas to reward children for memorizing scripture include:

Mystery Gift: Wrap a small gift for each child in gift wrap. Use one layer of paper for each Sunday in the unit. On the first Sunday, each child may choose a wrapped gift. Each following Sunday the child may remove one layer of gift wrap—*IF* he has learned the memory verse for that Sunday. When the child has learned all the verses in the unit and has unwrapped the gift, it is his to take home.

Memory Program: Arrange for the children to visit a local

nursing home where they can recite the scripture they have learned. The program may also include music.

Instead of going to a nursing home, the children may present the program in your local church. Or in children's church a memorized scripture passage may be recited as the Call to Worship, either individually or by a group as a choral-speaking.

Memorizing Bible passages can be exciting! Watch for ideas you can adapt to help your children hide God's Word in their hearts.

CHAPTER 11

Praying Is More than . . . "Fold Your Hands and Bow Your Heads"

Developing the ability to pray effectively is a lifelong task—but even the youngest child can begin. Children learn how to pray from example. The child who sees his children's church leaders pray when facing a difficulty, or rejoice over a blessing, has good models to follow. As children's church workers, our prayers should be deeply earnest, prayed whenever any need presents itself, expressed simply and briefly, and be a sincere expression of our faith in God and our desire to do His will. Children who regularly hear such prayers unconsciously absorb the essential elements of prayer.

The following principles will help to develop the habit of regular prayer.

1. *Build the children's faith in the God who hears and answers prayer.* Many times the Bible speaks of the importance of faith in our prayers (Eph. 6:13-18; James 5:15). Faith is not a

naive belief that God will give us what we ask just because we pray for it. Faith is an abiding trust in the goodness of God and His will for our lives. The Scriptures shows that God answers prayers in at least three ways. At times, He grants our request, as He did when Hannah prayed for a child (1 Samuel 1). Sometimes His answer is "Not now," or "Wait," as when He answered Job's prayers. Or God's will may be different from what we would choose for ourselves, so His answer may be "No!" An example of a negative answer is God's response to Jesus' prayer in the Garden of Gethsemane that He be spared from the agony of the Cross. The Cross was a part of God's plan of redemption, and God's answer was "No." Although the answer may not be what we would like at that moment, we accept God's answer as His will for us at that time.

This is a difficult concept for children to understand. The following illustration may help you explain it.

"Suppose your mother is baking cookies when you come home from school. They smell so good you can't wait to taste them. You ask for one and your mother says, 'Yes, you may have one.' When you ask for another one, your mother says, 'Wait until supper. I don't want you to spoil your appetite.' At supper you eat two more cookies. When you ask for thirds, your mother says, 'No. Three cookies are enough for one day.'"

Point out that God is much wiser than we are. He answers our prayers in the way that is best for us.

2. *Help the children develop the habit of praying whenever and wherever they feel a need.* Prayer should be a spontaneous and natural reaction. Children should feel as free to talk with God as they do with their parents or friends. Teach the children that they can pray at any time and at any place.

3. *Teach the children that prayer includes responsibility.* Whenever we pray, we must do our part to help God answer the prayer. We have no right to ask for God's protection and then live

carelessly. Prayer is a partnership, a covenant. When we pray, we often find that God points out something for us to do.

4. *Teach the children the value of having a regular time and place for prayer.* Having a special time and place for prayer encourages the regular practice of talking with God. The time may be in the early morning, at bedtime, at mealtime, or at any other time that is convenient. Sunday School and children's church also provide opportunities for prayer.

There is no contradiction in saying that God is available at all times and then planning a specific time for prayer. The latter enables us to live in close relationship with Him, the former encourages us to call on Him wherever and whenever we need His help.

5. *Use scripture to teach what God says about prayer.* God invites us to come boldly to Him (Heb. 4:16). Children can learn the joy of sharing their lives with God through prayer. Sometimes, however, there are hindrances. A lack of confidence or simply not knowing what to say may cause shyness. Children need to know we do not impress God with well-phrased prayers. He values the sincere, humble expression of our praise and needs. Some children may feel unable to put their needs into words. Help them realize that even adults don't always know how to say what they feel. That is when the Holy Spirit prays with and for us.

The best way to help children learn to pray is to start them praying. Try these suggestions to involve children in prayer time:

• Stand in a circle and join hands as the children pray for each other.

• Make a prayer chart. Invite the children to share prayer requests. Have several children offer sentence prayers.

• Have a time of silent prayer when each child offers his own requests. "Thought prayer" is praying without saying words aloud. Those not accustomed to praying in this manner will need direction. In a statement or two, the leader directs the thoughts of the group to a specific area of concern, then allows a brief time for each child to pray silently about that need. Example: "Think of a temptation you are facing or often face. Ask God to help you overcome it. (Silence) Think of a time when Jesus asked God to help Him know what to do. Thank God because He also helps us know what to do. (Silence) Amen." Close the prayer time by having the children sing a prayer chorus.

• Have the children write their prayer requests on slips of paper. Collect these slips in an offering plate. Pass the plate again and let each child who wishes take a slip of paper and pray for the request during prayer time. He may take the slip home and pray for the request until the following Sunday.

• Let those who are hesitant to pray aloud write out a prayer in their own words and read it as the others bow their heads.

• When the children attend adult worship, ask the pastor to pray particularly for them.

• Have the children close their eyes and sing a prayer chorus or a song that expresses their needs or concerns.

• Divide the children into pairs. Have one child pray for his partner, then let his partner pray for him.

• Ask the pastor to visit children's church to pray for the children. Or choose a senior citizen to come to the service and lead in prayer. Select one who can pray in children's language.

• Vary prayer time to keep this time of communion with God fresh and effective.

Children are forming many habits that will influence the rest of their lives. It is essential they be taught the habit of regular prayer. As leaders in children's church we share both the privilege and the responsibility of helping them discover the power of prayer.

12

Storytelling Can Be Learned

Children love stories that are told well. A good storyteller can paint a word picture so vividly the listener can't miss it. This ability is lying dormant within most of us. It may be buried under inhibitions, but it can be developed.

Bible stories are an important part of children's church. But unless you know *how* to make a story come alive, even the most exciting Bible story may be dull.

Here are some pointers to help you sharpen your storytelling.

1. Choose stories carefully. Stories can instruct, give information, motivate to action, solve problems, or entertain. Decide what you want to do, then choose a story to accomplish your purpose. When you use children's church curriculum, the story is usually already selected for you.

2. Plan your story. As you read the story, imagine the setting and action. Notice especially the characters and the sounds and feelings that surround them. Then make an outline of the story.

A story has four essential parts: introduction, plot, climax, and conclusion.

The purpose of the introduction is to grab the hearer's attention. A good introduction will make the children want to hear more. In the first few sentences, introduce the characters, begin the plot, and get the action underway. Set your scene and then let the characters introduce the story for you. Save details until the child's attention has been captured. Never throw away your introduction by beginning the story before the children are ready to listen. Sing a song, tell a joke, or have conversation, but wait for just the right moment to begin your story.

A good story has a plot that moves. Once the action has begun, its course needs to be direct. Highlight the action verbs that move your story along. Remember, children like action.

The climax is the high point of the story. It is the moment of discovery. It should reflect the purpose or application of the story. Eliminate anything that weakens this crucial moment.

A brief, satisfying ending should conclude the story. Don't tack on a moral. A well-constructed story does not need this to bring out the lesson. A moral says, "Since you're not smart enough to understand, I'll have to tell you what it's all about." If the story has not pointed out the truth by the climax, an added preachment will do little good.

Practice Your Delivery

Don't try to tell a story until you are comfortable with it. Practice it privately. During your early practice periods you may be a bit hazy about some of the incidents, or perhaps appropriate words will fail to come in certain places. If beginning and ending the story are hard, memorize the first and last sentences to insure a strong opening and finish. When you are ready, ask another adult to listen to and critique your presentation.

Even if your friend is lavish with praise, more practice is needed. You must be so familiar with the story that you can concentrate on watching the children's faces for responses. Only when you experience the freedom that comes from knowing the story well, can you give yourself to interpretation. PRACTICE is the price that must be paid for skill in storytelling.

How to Tell a Story

Use your voice. Let it create the mood as well as say the words. For example, suppose you are telling the story of the good Samaritan and say,

"The traveler was going along the road all alone. It was dark and the man was afraid . . ."

Use a low tone of voice as if telling a secret. This gives the idea of darkness, fear, and danger. When you come to the part where the traveler is attacked, raise your voice and speak rapidly. Let your voice convey the idea of the attack.

When characters in the story speak, imitate their voices. Let your voice express your feelings.

Use your eyes. They can help you tell a story by showing how you feel about what happens in the story. Direct eye contact can hold the children's attention. It makes them feel you are telling the story especially for them. Each child feels that you know he is there, listening.

Use the pause. Silence creates suspense. Pause just before a moment of discovery.

Use the whisper. Drop your voice to tell a secret, emphasize a point, or introduce a "meanwhile" scene—"Meanwhile, back at the Jerusalem palace, Herod was plotting a wicked plan." A whisper, like a pause, creates suspense.

Use sounds in the story. Sound effects help communicate action and hold attention. Imagine what television programs and radio shows would be like without them.

If you tell about a train coming, make the sound of the locomotive.

If someone is knocking at the door, rap on a table or wall.

Imitate the sounds of the wind blowing, the meow of a kitten, the barnyard sounds. Add sounds to the word pictures you paint.

Use your whole body. Study your story carefully to discover ways to use gestures to make it come alive. Stand on tiptoes as Zacchaeus must have done in order to see Jesus. Kneel down to look for the lost coin. Walk with Jesus as He goes to the Temple. Run for your life as you escape from the Egyptians.

Involve Children in Active Listening

Children listen better when they have a reason to pay attention. Involve them in action listening by giving them something to watch for.

Here are some storytelling techniques to help get and keep attention.

Secret word game. Write a word you will use quite a few times while you are telling the story. Place the paper in an envelope or a mysteriously decorated box. Before you start the story, show the children the envelope or box. Explain that it contains a secret word. Tell the children it is a word you will use often. You may give a small clue such as, "It is not the name of the person." Tell them to listen carefully because during activity time, each child will write down what he thinks the secret word is, and sign his name. Each child who guesses the "word" correctly will receive a small prize.

Quiz board. Before telling the story, tell the children that after the story you will choose three to five children to be members of the "QUIZ BOARD." The other children get to ask the Quiz Board questions about the story. Everyone must listen. Some will *ask questions* and others will *answer them.*

After 10 or 15 questions have been answered, choose a new Quiz Board. Continue the game as long as interest is maintained.

Listening sheets. Prepare a simple activity sheet for the children to complete during the story. Use fill-in-the-blanks or multiple-choice questions.

Visuals. Visual aids help to hold attention and aid the child's understanding. Stories are always more interesting when you use props. There are two rules for using objects: (1) they should relate to the story; and (2) if you don't want the children to touch the object, don't bring it.

News reporter. Have two or more workers present the story as a newscast. One person can tell what happened, the second can interview the children for their reactions or comments.

The story is central in children's church. It *is* the message. Your goal as you tell a story is to change lives. Before you can do that, however, you must get and hold the children's attention. When a child can predict what you will do and how you will do it, look for ways to give variety. The ideas above are designed to spark *your creativity.*

Enjoy yourself when you tell a story. The storyteller's attitude is crucial. When he enjoys and appreciates the story himself, the children will relax and drink in the message.

I must not interfere with any child
—I have been told. Nor bend his will to
mine, or try to shape him through some
mold of thought.

Naturally, as a flower, he must
unfold.

Yet flowers have the discipline of
wind and rain, and though I know it
gives the gardner much pain, I've seen
him use his pruning shears to gain more
strength and beauty for some blossoms
bright. And he would do whatever he
thought right.

I do not know—yet it does seem to
me—that only weeds unfold just
naturally.

—Author unknown

CHAPTER 13

Keys to Positive Discipline

A children's church session is seldom a place of perfect order and obedience. However, good behavior is important! One child's misconduct can interrupt the session and turn a well-planned service into a disaster.

Adults enjoy their work with children when there is good discipline. Visitors are impressed with children who are attentive and interested. But these are not the *prime* reasons for maintaining good discipline.

Good discipline is necesssary for children to learn respect for themselves and others. We need to help children see they are damaging themselves and each other through bad bahavior. This damage may be either physical or emotional, or both. The ability to cope with behavior problems is an important qualification for a children's church leader.

Discipline—What Is It?

Discipline must be understood properly if it is to be practiced effectively. Many define discipline as punishment. However, the two words are not synonymous. Discipline is a learning process. Punishment is merely one technique used to correct behavior problems. To be most effective, punishment should be a logical consequence of the offending behavior.

The lessons of discipline are not taught in one or two encounters. The normal child continues to test long-established rules periodically. The goal of discipline is to move children toward self-control rather than external control.

The Leader's Role in Discipline

The adult leader is qualified to discipline children only when he is disciplined himself. Since discipline is a teaching-learning process, the teacher must practice what he is teaching. When his authority as teacher/leader is challenged, he must respond as a disciplined, mature Christian. An undisciplined reaction only escalates the problem.

It is also important for the adult leader to *know* each child in his group. This gives him insight into the causes of inappropriate behavior. A leader can get to know a child by visiting the home to see him in his family setting, watching the child at play, listening to him, and making note of his successes and failures. How the child relates to his peers and how he feels about himself are crucial factors in his behavior.

Finally, the leader is not qualified to discipline a child unless he has prayed for him. Prayer can unlock doors of understanding that otherwise remain closed. Pray for any child who has problems. Without mentioning the child by name, enlist others to pray with you. Prayer does make a difference.

Plan to Avoid Problems

In discipline, an ounce of prevention is worth *more* than a pound of cure. Here are some suggestions that will improve the learning environment and lessen the occurrence of discipline problems.

Be a refreshed worker. A good rest on Saturday night is the best prescription to insure that you are mentally alert on Sunday morning. If you are physically tired, the chances are that children's church will be negatively affected.

Enlist adequate personnel. This is a major factor in retaining positive control of a group of children. Ideally, there should be one worker for every 8-10 children. Discipline problems decrease in direct proportion to a good leader-child ratio. Older teenagers may be used as helpers, with adequate adult supervision.

Provide a pleasant environment. A disorderly room invites disorderly behavior. A drab, crowded room with poor ventilation and uncomfortable furnishings will contribute to discipline problems.

Be prepared. You can be sure you will lose control of the children if you are inadequately prepared. Have a plan for every minute, but remain flexible enough to alter the procedure when your "best laid plans" don't work. When several children become disorderly, perhaps your teaching method is wrong. Children often misbehave when they are bored. Don't hesitate to drop an uninteresting game or project. Give the children frequent opportunities to change positions. Remember, the attention span of children is short. Having some alternative ideas at hand may save a session from becoming an unfortunate event.

Expect the children to behave. Children try to live up to your expectations of them. Never make statements like "I don't think Cheryl knows *how* to behave," or, "You can always expect Jimmy to talk." Don't give a child a bad reputation to live up to. When a problem arises, criticize the behavior, not the child.

Be positive in your approach. Say, "Walk quietly," rather than, "Don't run." "I see Mary is almost ready," is better than, "Shhhh, Mary. We can't start until you are quiet!" Statements such as, "I like the way David is sitting up straight," may cause other children to copy his behavior.

Watch for and reward children who are behaving. Children who behave often go unnoticed. If you spend all your energy on misbehaving children, some children who normally behave may misbehave just to gain your attention. Reward good behavior. Appropriate praise is one of the best discipline techniques at your disposal.

Establish eye contact. Know your material so well you can look at the children while interacting with them. This helps hold the child's attention and also gives you vital information about your children's reactions. If a child is misbehaving, eye contact is often sufficient to restore appropriate behavior.

Know your children by name. Children tend to cooperate more readily if they realize you know who they are. It also helps if you call a misbehaving child by name.

Let children suggest rules. Most children tend to respond better when they have helped make the guidelines. Rules should be based upon concern for others. Ask children to suggest "Do" rules. If they suggest "Don'ts," help them rephrase them positively. These rules should make good sense to the children and be as few in number as possible. Be sure the children clearly understand each rule. Be absolutely consistent in enforcing rules from week to week. Review the rules often to remind the regulars and inform newcomers. Print them on a poster and display where the boys and girls can see it.

Here are five rules one group made.
   A. Use inside voices.
   B. Take turns.
   C. One person speaks at a time.
   D. Listen to the leaders.
   E. Be kind.

Teach children to listen. Children need to learn good listening skills. Begin by talking about listening. Then discuss the conditions for good listening: (1) mind attentive; (2) ears open; (3) mouth closed; (4) hands quiet; (5) feet still; and (6) eyes on the leader. Prepare an attractive poster and use it to review as necessary. Help children discover that listening is "watching with their ears." They are to see what they can *learn* by listening.

Look for the Cause of Misbehavior

Many disruptive children are not "bad" but "hurt." Their misbehavior may be a way to express their inner feelings. Death, divorce, constant battling at home, or even something as harmless as moving to a new home and school can cause anger, hostility, or aggressiveness. When children have behavior problems, it is vital that you look beyond the action to its cause.

However, not all inappropriate behavior is the result of childhood trauma. Some children misbehave simply to get attention. Every children's worker knows children who are not loved or cared for at home, or who do not do well in school or sports. Such children may feel that negative attention is better than no attention at all. If attention is their need, give them the attention they crave in positive ways. Show them you like them. Accept them openly. Recognize their successes and minimize or ignore their failures.

Always look at past behavior patterns when you are looking for the cause of misbehavior. The "undisciplined" child has usually been disruptive for some time. The "hurt" child will have a sudden or gradual change in his behavior.

One hour in children's church will not solve all the troubled child's problems. However, it is significant. This may be his only encounter with God. However difficult it may be, you must show His love to the child. This does not mean you are to overlook the disruptive behavior. Your task is to discipline the child in love. Direct his actions through rewarding acceptable behavior and showing him how to act when he misbehaves. This is a tall order. Your only hope is to let GOD love the child through you.

Techniques for Handling Problems

One qualification for effective leadership is love. However, a leader who loves children can still have a children's church that is out of hand. Here are some techniques that will help you handle disruptive behavior when it does occur:

Be firm but affectionate. Studies show that children feel better if they are made to behave. Limits provide a sense of security. When a child oversteps a limit, try to find the cause. Do not expect simplistic answers. If possible, remove the cause and restore the child to appropriate behavior.

Learn to ignore nondisruptive behavior. Part of the skill of controlling children is knowing when not to respond. Ignoring minor attention-getting behavior may be the best way to handle a situation. This gives the child time to come to terms with his behavior, and does not reward it with your attention. If you react to every minor incident, you invite the children to "tease" you with their misbehavior.

Use praise generously. One of the best ways to correct and eliminate bad behavior is to compliment good behavior. Sincerely praise the efforts the children are making. Always be honest when you praise. Children will quickly see through flattery, and your praise will lose its effectiveness.

Watch the seating arrangements. Problems often arise because certain combinations of children are seated together. Try separating children who cannot control themselves if they sit together. Avoid scolding. Politely ask the children to change places, or have an adult join the group. One effective way to break up cliques is to have the children number off by twos. Make it seem like a game. For that session, all the twos sit in one area and the ones in another. This usually separates potential troublemaking groups.

Involve children. If some children become unruly, try to involve the whole group in meaningful activity. You may need to assign tasks. Be careful not to reward bad behavior.

If you are in the middle of a story and cannot switch to an activity, ask questions that require responses. Give the children something particular to listen for. Let them know a discussion will follow so they will want to be attentive.

Set up signals. Pointing, a nod, or a glance reminds misbehaving children that what they are doing should be controlled. Often misconduct can be stopped in its early stages through the use of these kinds of personal signals. If a signal from a distance is not enough, try moving next to the disruptive child. If you are sitting next to an unruly child, put your arm around him. This shows the child you care about him and also helps control his behavior.

Special attention. If a child continually exhibits inappropriate behavior, find time to talk with him privately. This allows you to explore his needs. Let him know you consider him an important part of the group. A private conference will avoid putting the child on the defensive in front of his friends. When a child is corrected in front of the entire group, everyone gets involved. Children will sometimes feel sympathy for the disciplined child and take his side. These feelings may cause further misbehavior. If you discover the child is starved for attention, arrange ways to recognize him for good rather than bad behavior.

Gain control. When a large number of children misbehave or become rebellious, stop all activity until order is restored.

Remove chronic disrupters. On rare occasions you may need to remove a child from the rest of the group. This should be a last resort. When it happens be certain the child understands: (1) the reason he is being removed; (2) that you still love him; (3) that you are sad that he misbehaved and had to be removed; and (4) what he must do to be reinstated in the group. Always let the child rejoin the group when he corrects his behavior.

Don't threaten unless you intend to carry out the threat—and don't promise unless you can fulfill the promise.

Discipline, with God's Help

It is difficult to be helpful and healing when your session seems to be falling apart. It is especially hard when your children's church is understaffed and you cannot give the individual attention a child needs. One hour a week is a short time to try to form a loving relationship with a child who has a behavior problem.

However, don't let the difficulties defeat you. Remember, God is the true Leader of your children's church. You are doing His work. You can discipline with His help.

The miracle is that God loves and reaches out to children through people like you and me. Love the children enough to know when a child is hurting. Then act in the name of Jesus who loves him.

HOW OLD?

"Dear Mother," said the little maid,
  "Please whisper it to me . . .
Before I am a Christian
  How old ought I to be?"

"How old ought you to be, dear child,
  Before you can love me?"
"I've always loved you, Mummy dear,
  Since I was tiny, wee."

"I love you now and always will,"
  The little daughter said,
And on her mother's shoulder hid
  Her golden, curly head.

"How old, my daughter, must you be
  Before you trust my care?"
"O Mother dear, I do, I do,
  I trust you everywhere."

"Then you can be a Christian too;
  Don't wait 'till you are grown.
Tell Jesus now you come to Him
  To be His very own."

And so the little maid knelt down,
  And said, "Lord, if I may,
I'd like to be a Christian now."
  He answered, "Yes, today!"

—Author unknown

14

How to Lead a Child to Christ

The Need

In today's world, children need the security that only faith in God can give. How can we help boys and girls come to know God as a real Person in their lives?

The disciples thought adults were more important than children. They rebuked the mothers for bothering Jesus when they brought their children to Him. But Jesus was indignant at His disciples' action. He said, "Let the little children come to me, and do not hinder them, for the kingdom of God belongs to such as these" (Mark 10:14, NIV).

The attitude of minimizing the importance of children did not die with the disciples. Even today some belittle the conversion and faith of children. They feel it is more profitable to spend their time ministering to adults. However, studies show that the years between 9 and 14 are the "six golden years for God." Many of the church's most productive workers received Christ when they were children.

Dwight L. Moody is said to have returned from a meeting with a report of two and one half conversions. "I suppose you mean two adults and one child," said his host.

"No," said Mr. Moody, "I mean two children and one adult. You see, the children can give their whole lives, but the adult has only half of his life left to give."

If Adam Clarke had been saved at 74 rather than at 4, we would be without his Bible commentary. If Jonathan Edwards had become a Christian at 80 instead of 8, we would have been without one of America's great preachers. If Matthew Henry had been converted at 70 instead of 11, another great commentary would be missing. Never make the mistake of treating lightly the salvation of children. If they are won, their lives are saved for God's service.

Leader Preparation

Only when a leader experiences the reality of God in his own life can he share it with children. Children's church is a special kind of teaching—a kind of preaching and encouraging children to accept Jesus as Savior. You must know Christ as your personal Savior to do this kind of teaching.

The leader must have a clear understanding of what the child needs to know in order to appreciate the plan of salvation. This message must be simple, yet complete.

The leader must be guided by God. It is the Holy Spirit who convicts and draws the child to God. If the child feels guilty only because of human convincing, rather than because of the conviction of the Holy Spirit, his "conversion" will not be genuine. Actually, this kind of man-made decision may be harmful.

Evangelizing a Child

At a boys' and girls' camp, one little girl ran up to me and excitedly exclaimed, "I've been saved three times! I got saved at camp again this year. Every year at camp I get saved." Her testimony is not unique.

To many workers in children's church the term *evangelism* refers only to those attempts made to secure a personal commitment from the child. Such a commitment must be included in a definition, but to stop there is to do grave injustice to the program of child evangelism. The term might better be defined as a process in which crisis conversion is preceded by careful Christian teaching and is followed by nurture, which helps the child become established in his Christian experience.

This idea of "process" does not minimize our belief that a crisis experience is necessary. It simply underscores the fact that conversion is most likely to survive when it is built upon a foundation of sound Christian teaching and nurtured by a continued program of discipleship.

Know the Child

What do you know about each child in your group? Do you know the home environment? Do you have a relationship with the parents that allows you to discuss the child's spiritual growth? What signs does the child give that show his stage of spiritual awareness?

To be an effective children's evangelist, you must know the children as individuals (no two alike) as well as their general age-level characteristics. (These age-level characteristics are discussed fully in age-group texts.) Background and training affect the child's readiness to respond to Christ.

The Invitation

Some children's church leaders feel that the plan of salvation should be presented in every session. *Leading Children in Worship* does not follow this plan. Certain units or sessions within units are more evangelistic in nature. Suggestions for giving an invitation are written into these sessions. However, each child is an individual and progresses toward spiritual awareness at his own rate. Watch carefully for signs of a Spirit-awakened hunger. Talk personally with the child about his need, even though no group invitation is given.

It is not difficult to get children to respond if you exert a little emotional pressure. However, a decision for Christ founded *solely* on emotion is a poor basis for a Christian life. Don't settle for emotional manipulation in an evangelistic invitation for children. They can know real conviction. Children know right from wrong. They are aware of their sins. Let the Holy Spirit do His own work.

Before you give an invitation, make sure all workers know what to do when children respond. Once the plan has been established, you will always be ready for times when the Holy Spirit comes in an unusual way. Assign specific workers the responsibility of directing planned activities for those children who do not respond to the invitation. Assign other workers to take those who respond to a quiet place to pray. Generally this plan works better than trying to keep the children quiet while those who have responded are praying.

When a boy or girl comes to pray, ask his name if you do not already know it. Calling the child by name, ask WHY he has come. He may be at the altar for a variety of reasons. Let the child state his need. This will keep you from praying for him to be "saved" if he has come to pray for his sick mother, a friend, or even his pet.

Sometimes when children come to the altar, it is because the Holy Spirit has checked them. They are "walking in the light." Be ready to explain how the Lord leads us day by day. Show your happiness that the child is walking close enough to the Lord to hear His voice. Share the fact that this is how all Christians become stronger.

Be careful not to use symbols the child cannot understand.

"Accept Jesus as your Savior" or "Ask God to forgive you" are statements the child can take literally and will not need to be changed as he grows older.

Be personal. Use the child's name as you talk with him, and as you pray with him. As he reads the Bible verses, have him put his own name in the verse. For example:

"For God so loved Johnny that he gave his one and only Son, that if Johnny believes in him, Johnny shall not perish but have eternal life" (John 3:16, NIV).

Use your Bible. *Really Living* gives a step-by-step plan for children. A *Leader's Guide* is also available with further helps. A simple outline from *Really Living* is:

1. God LOVES YOU and wants you to REALLY LIVE (John 3:16 and John 10:10).
2. You have sinned (Rom. 3:23).
3. Jesus died for our sins (Rom. 5:8).
4. You must repent:

    Admit you have sinned;

    Feel sorry for your sins;

    Be willing to quit sinning;

    ASK God to forgive you (1 John 1:9).
5. Receive Jesus as your Savior (Rev. 3:20; John 1:12).
6. Pray, and have the child pray too. It is better if the child will pray in his own words. If not, have him repeat after you a simple prayer such as:

    God, I admit I have sinned and I am sorry for what I have done. Please forgive me.

    I believe Jesus died for me. I now accept Him as my own Savior.

    Help me to obey You every day. Thank You for forgiving me and making me Your child. Amen.

After he has prayed, ask the child what the Lord has done for him. If he cannot answer clearly, refer back to the Bible. Ask such questions as, "What did God say He would do? What did you ask Him to do?" Conversion is God's supernatural work and the Holy Spirit can witness to the heart of a child. Close your work at the altar with a brief prayer in which you give thanks for what the Lord has done.

Follow Up

Follow-up is the continuing nurturing process that helps the new Christian become established. It begins immediately after conversion. Give some suggestions on how to grow as a Christian. Point out that Satan tempts new Christians to do wrong and turn away from the Lord. Stress that Jesus is stronger than the devil, but we are not. That is why we need God's help. He helps us when we read the Bible and pray. Emphasize that we can pray for strength each time we feel tempted.

If you used *Really Living,* give the child a copy to take home. Tell him that when the devil tempts him to doubt what the Lord has done, he should read the Bible verses in the booklet again. If you did not use *Really Living,* help the child find and mark the verses in his Bible, or copy them and give them to him. Give the child a devotional book, such as *Living as a Christian,* to help him begin growing.

Contact the new convert again within a few days. Phone, write, or visit him at home. If you see the child in person, talk with him privately. It may embarrass him if you speak to him in front of others.

When the child feels comfortable with the idea, call in the home and help him explain to his parents what happened. Use a copy of *Really Living* to explain to the parents how their child accepted Jesus Christ as Savior. In some cases, the parent may want to receive Christ at the close of the explanation.

The age when a child is ready to accept Christ varies widely according to his background, his mental and spiritual maturity, and other personal differences. The Holy Spirit alone knows when a child should be invited to accept Christ. We can, however, pray that God will keep us sensitive to the spiritual needs of the children under our care. We can watch our boys and girls closely so we will recognize when they are ready to open their hearts to the Savior. There is no greater joy for a children's worker than to lead a child to Christ!

I Led a Child to Christ

Today, I led a child to Christ,
  A child unfettered by earth's care,
And all unmarred by scarlet sin,
  How clear and simple was his prayer!
"Forgive me, God, for wrongs I've done,
  And keep me always straight and true,
I want to serve You all my life,
  And do just what You'd have me do."
Today, I brought a child to Christ,
  And many precious days and years
To spend in service to the King;
  A life free from regretful tears—
An open mind to learn the way—
  A voice that will not shun to speak
The truth—a heart to pray—
  And youthful zeal the lost to seek.

I thank, Thee, God, for granting me
  Wisdom to read upon his face
His readiness to come to Thee,
  His willingness to trust Thy grace.
Whatever treasures may be mine
  To keep and cherish on life's way,
None shall outshine this brightest one—
  I led a CHILD to Christ today!

                    —*Kathryn Blackburn Peck*

PART V

THE CHALLENGE—Go for It!

A Boy in Tarsus

THERE WAS A BOY IN TARSUS. You
probably wouldn't have paid much
attention to him, this skinny Jewish
lad, with the questions in his eyes.
Perhaps he stood on the corner with a
gang of other boys, bragging about his
father being a Roman citizen, or how
he could weave goat hair into tent
cloth! "He's an enthusiastic little
fellow!" you might have said, and
passed on.

THERE WAS A BOY IN TARSUS. The
Roman eagles flapped in the wind over
the earth; Caesar's legions and Caesar's
battle galleys commanded the seas and
the lands of the world. But this boy in
Tarsus was more important than all
that! The far, dim future was spiked
with cathedral pinnacles; and under
them was written not Caesar but the
name of the lad from Tarsus!

THERE WAS A BOY IN TARSUS.
Immortality walked the streets of that
city! He was a restless boy. The dreams
stirred and quivered in him. There was
a kingdom on his sky, and a voice in

his sleep for there was a war in the universe, between Satan and God, for the boy's soul!

THERE WAS A BOY IN TARSUS. But there was more than a boy. There was a wide kingdom, greater than a thousand Romes. There was a poem beginning: "Though I speak with the tongues of men and of angels. . . ." There were books: Romans, Corinthians, Galatians, Ephesians, Philippians, Colossians, Titus! A new era in human history, called Christian, was there in Tarsus, walking around in a boy with his hands in his pockets, and the questions in his eyes! Sometimes boys are awfully important!

—Lon Woodrum

Used by permission.

CHAPTER 15

You Can Make the Difference

When a boy or girl thrusts his small hand in yours, it may be smeared with chocolate ice cream, or grimy from petting a dog, and there may be a wart under the right thumb and a bandage on the little finger.

But the most important thing about his hands is that they are the hands of the future. These are the hands that someday may hold a Bible, or a colt revolver. They may play the church piano, or spin a gambling wheel, they may gently dress a leper's wound, or tremble wretchedly uncontrolled by an alcoholic mind.

Right now the hand is in yours. It asks for help and guidance. It represents a full-fledged personality in miniature, to be respected as a separate individual whose day-by-day growth into Christian adulthood is your responsibility.

—Author unknown

Jesus loved children. When He wanted to teach a lesson in faith and humility, He used a child as the example (Matt. 18:2).

At another time He said, "Let the little children come to me, and do not hinder them, for the kingdom of God belongs to such as these" (Luke 18:16, NIV). How do you feel about children? Do you have a strong inner desire to help bring them to Jesus? To nurture and guide them until they, "being rooted and established in love . . . become mature, attaining to the whole measure of the fullness of Christ"? (Eph. 3:17; 4:13, NIV). If you do, then look carefully at children's church as a possible area for ministry.

Workers for children's church are often in short supply. Frankly, the task is not easy. It requires time and effort for preparation. It takes a firm commitment to your goals, because not everyone in the church will agree with what you do. But don't let the potential difficulties keep you from enjoying the reward of knowing that you have had a part in bringing the children in your church to Jesus.

Does God want you to minister through children's church? You must decide. If He does, accept the challenge. You can make the difference in the lives of boys and girls!